THE FULL CATASTROPHE

THE FULL CATASTROPHE

STORIES FROM WHEN LIFE WAS SO BAD IT WAS FUNNY

Rebecca Huntley + Sarah Macdonald

Hardie Grant

BOOKS

Published in 2019 by Hardie Grant Books,
an imprint of Hardie Grant Publishing

Hardie Grant Books (Melbourne)
Building 1, 658 Church Street
Richmond, Victoria 3121

Hardie Grant Books (London)
5th & 6th Floors
52–54 Southwark Street
London SE1 1UN

hardiegrantbooks.com

A catalogue record for this
book is available from the
NATIONAL
LIBRARY   National Library of Australia
OF AUSTRALIA

The Full Catastrophe
ISBN 978 1 74379 545 3

10 9 8 7 6 5 4 3 2 1

Cover design by Alissa Dinallo
Typeset in 11/15 pt Minion Pro by Post Pre-press Group, Brisbane
Printed by McPherson's Printing Group, Maryborough, Victoria

The paper this book is printed on is certified against the Forest
Stewardship Council® Standards. FSC® promotes environmentally
responsible, socially beneficial and economically viable management of
the world's forests.

Dedicated to catastrophisers everywhere …
may you rise above it with a smile.

And to our husbands, Jonathan and Daniel,
who manage to stay calm in the face of almost anything.

REBECCA HUNTLEY is one of Australia's best-known social researchers. She has a PhD in politics, three children, and goes to bed at 8 pm most nights. She is a writer and broadcaster, and the presenter of *The History Listen* on the ABC's RN every week.

SARAH MACDONALD is an author, facilitator and presenter of *Weekend Nightlife* on ABC Radio. Her bestselling memoir, *Holy Cow*, is still travelling the world more than she is. She has two teenagers and a dog and goes to bed at 2 am.

Sarah and Rebecca text a lot in the middle of the day.

Contents

Part 4: Heart Problems

Part 5: Completely Catastrophic

What are two nice girls doing in a book like this?

WE ALL KNOW one person who somehow flies golden through life. That person who was born beautiful, wealthy, talented and smart, and who does everything well. That individual who lands great jobs, carries them out superbly, and has never ever humiliated themselves at work, in relationships or in public. How we want to hate that person. But, bloody hell, we can't even do that because they are usually so damn untouched by life that they are glowingly charming and always kind to animals.

Infuriating.

Luckily, we don't know anyone like that. And even if that person did exist, this book is not for them. It's for you and your friends and family. Those mortals who have stuff-ups, cock-ups and calamities. The real people.

As we grow older, we realise many things. We realise how dysfunctional our bodies can be and how we should have appreciated them more when we were hotter. We discover that success often goes to the best operator and not the most decent and hard working. We learn that life is often unfair. And we also discover that our lives will be full of minor catastrophes, major stuff-ups and horrific humiliations.

First-world problems mostly. But problems none the less.

Our show, *The Full Catastrophe*, came about because Sarah has a terrible memory. She'd somehow forgotten terrible moments in her semi-charmed life of being a bestselling writer, radio broadcaster and mother. So when much of her life fell apart a few years ago, she found herself floundering blindly and gasping in shock. Rebecca is good in a crisis (well, at least, in other people's). She cooked meals for Sarah and delivered them with Italian tablecloths and healthy desserts. She covered for her at work. But most of all, she let Sarah turn that frown upside down. One day, when Sarah was telling Rebecca the latest intimate and disgusting details about death and disaster, Rebecca started to laugh. She laughed because it was all too much. She laughed at the horror. She laughed because it was so ridiculous, there was nothing else to do. Sarah needed that laugh like a beacon in the darkness, and she followed that laugh to the promised land of getting over herself.

And after that coming together in the soup of sorrow, Rebecca and Sarah found they really loved each other and when two people really love each other, they can make a baby. And after a long labour, a lot of screaming and swearing and even more drugs, *The Full Catastrophe* storytelling event was born.

We originally wanted to call the show *Clusterfuck*, because there are times in our lives when all the messy bits and pieces, the stresses and competing passions, interests and demands combine to form a shit-storm so epic that it must simply be greeted in the foetal position. But we are nice ladies who swear far too much, so we resisted. At our first *Full Catastrophe* at Giant Dwarf in Redfern, Sydney, we expected, well, a catastrophe. We'd never hosted an event like this. We'd never tried to be funny in front of an audience. But we had an inkling that a catastrophe shared is a catastrophe diverted, and we hoped there would be great solace in sharing disasters with other people. As we expected, the event was messy and silly. Rebecca was sick and combined heavy duty flu medicine with cheap champagne, which meant she dramatically overshared on one orifice-involved detail in her catastrophic story. But something else happened. We found that *The Full Catastrophe* was akin to a group hug, a cheap group-therapy session with alcohol, and a joyful up-yours to dark times. We had asked others – more successful, famous and admired people – to share their disasters and, my god, it felt so good to hear these wonderful people generously share their major stuff-ups. We felt we'd finally found a club that would take us.

Every story that has been told at a *Full Catastrophe* event has made us laugh, gasp and wipe the tears of joy and sadness from our eyes. Yet we always get the biggest thrill from the reaction of the audience. At the end of one event, a woman came up to us, crying with pleasure. We thought she wanted to gloat in gratuitous thrill that these fabulous personalities had exposed their messy bits. But no. She blubbered, 'Thank you for making me feel my disastrous life is actually okay.'

'Our pleasure, grasshopper,' we said.

The cult was born.

And that's what this is about. We recognise that many of us in these pages are extremely lucky in life, but we learn that none of us is immune from disaster. In fact, we are often a hair's breadth away from it. And while some awful things cannot be laughed at, many can and should be. Sometimes a catastrophe is of our own making. Sometimes we put ourselves in uncomfortable situations. Deborah Knight, Cathy Wilcox and Emma Alberici travelled with children. Clem Bastow went on a quest for love and tempted fate. Sometimes the catastrophe comes to us in the form of the birth of a child (Annabel Crabb), or the death of a loved one (Sarah), or just the act of walking out the front door and into an IKEA store (Rebecca). In this collection, there are family catastrophes, disasters at work (Kate McClymont is the toughest chick we know) and in love, disasters with fruit (or is an avocado a vegetable, Bernard Salt?), and crises that are so insane they defy description. While some of us court catastrophe and some of us like to catastrophise, most often disasters are beyond our control. We are at the mercy of the love we feel for others, which can place us in perilous situations. (What were you thinking, Robbie Buck?)

So come with us, dear connoisseur of human failings, as we traipse through a landscape of humour and fiasco. We hope you read these stories and feel better about yourself, your life and your decisions. And know, in your heart, that this too shall pass.

Part 1

Domestic Drama

Wrong Way Go Back

Annabel Crabb

P EOPLE HAVE BABIES all the time. It is among the least original things a human being can do, apart from dying and wearing ironic T-shirts. Far more hopeless people than Jeremy and I do it all the time; I feel, defensively, that I should point that out before telling this story.

We were in our mid-thirties. We lived in London and held down capable jobs. We had conceived a baby, after that customary awkward interregnum that confronts thirty-something couples when they pull that strategic handbrake turn from years of applying substantial ingenuity to the task of not getting pregnant, and start applying it to achieve the opposite result. It's then they discover that it's harder than one always thought.

We'd already encountered a small-scale debacle by the time I was in my ninth month of pregnancy. The public hospital up the road from us was a place called the Whittington. Its emblem was a black cat. Fine; I'm not superstitious. The hospital dates back to the 1400s, and survived the Great Fire of London and several name changes over that time, having at different stages been known as the City of London Lying-in Hospital for Married Ladies and St Luke's Hospital for Lunatics. I liked all these aspects of my proposed ante-natal care.

But I cooled on the place when we arrived for a look at the labour ward and found that many of the facility's original fifteenth-century features remained. We were instructed that if I wanted pillows, I would have to bring them. I was planning a water birth, having read that babies can remain submerged indefinitely when born into water, on account of receiving their oxygen through the umbilical cord. I was keen to see this phenomenon for myself. I reasoned there would not be much else very entertaining in the general process of squeezing a large baby out of an unfeasibly snug aperture. You have to make your own fun, after all.

So I fled the Whittington and booked myself, at the last minute, into a birth centre in North London. Miles and miles from our home, it was a free-standing birth centre with lovely midwives called names like Rowan and Elderflower (it's possible I am embroidering this).

The birth centre had CD players and comfy chairs and a kettle and big queen-sized beds where your partner could stay over. And it had birth pools. In terms of pain relief, though, you were looking at ice cubes and scented candles, and that was about it. The midwives explained that in the event of complications, we'd have to jump in an ambulance. These seemed like reasonable terms.

A week before the baby was due, our friend James came round for dinner. This may, in retrospect, have been an error. James is a mathematical genius with a taste for conversation and fine wine. I went to bed at ten. Jeremy, taking one for the team, stayed up late with James and several bottles of red. He stumbled into bed at ten to one. And at ten past one, my waters broke.

Now, all the books agree that in the weeks before you give birth, everybody needs to get some rest. It's a pretty ropey business, having a baby, and it works best when everyone is calm and well-slept. I cannot find any reference in the published literature to the ramifications where one party has only been asleep a couple of hours and the other one has David Boon blood-alcohol levels, but I have my suspicions.

'Jeremy!' I hissed, rolling over and jabbing him savagely. 'I need a towel! My waters broke!' He turned over and gave me a drunken pat.

'Darling,' he drawled, 'you shall have all the towels you require.' And then he went back to sleep. I couldn't wake him again after that.

I lay there for a while, timing contractions and wondering whether this whole thing hadn't been a poor idea. After a couple of hours, I lumbered off and ran a bath, which I was then unable to clamber out of. I summoned Jeremy in the end by hurling bars of soap and bottles of shampoo at the bathroom door. He rallied brilliantly, I must say, considering his handicaps.

We faced a few hurdles, though. For one, we didn't have a car, it was 4.30 am, and London taxis have a policy of not carrying women in labour. Also, we hadn't packed a bag. This is a real rookie error, I know, but in my defence, the baby wasn't due for another whole week and I like to work to deadline.

I developed an urgent need to make green tomato chutney. So I set about doing that, while Jeremy stumbled out to find one of those GoGet cars. Looking back on it, I am hopeful that he was merely horribly hungover by this point, and not still technically shickered. He also packed a bag, very kindly, and as dawn broke we set off.

It became clear almost immediately that neither of us had much of an idea of how to get to the birth centre. It was miles away, in an unfamiliar part of London. We seemed to have somehow taken a route that visited every speed hump in North London. We drove grimly, in silence. 'Shall we put some music on?' suggested Jeremy at one point. I opened the hospital bag he'd packed. It contained muesli, plates and Neil Young CDs. I actively dislike Neil Young. This was going to be a long day.

Things improved sharply when we arrived at the birth centre, which was – as imagined – a calm and pillow-strewn haven of friendliness and efficiency. I had a piece of toast and hopped into a delightful warm birth pool. Matters progressed. Jeremy was doing all the back rubbing and muttered encouragement. What could possibly go wrong from here?

Well. The midwife – after checking the progress of my labours – had some awkward news. 'I'm so sorry,' she said. 'I have no idea how we failed to pick this up earlier, but your baby is in the breech position. Now, I can deliver a breech baby – I've done it before – but this is your first baby and I'm afraid I would have to advise evacuating you to hospital.' The thought of hauling myself out of this delightful bath and clambering into an ambulance was not attractive. But to imperil the baby's wellbeing purely because of my laziness seemed a poor way to kick off our relationship. So within ten minutes I was strapped to a plank in the back of an ambulance, streaking towards yet another hospital, Jeremy zooming along behind in the hire car.

On our arrival at this new hospital, it became clear quite swiftly that my vague plans of popping back into a bath and resuming my work did not square with the plans of the awaiting medical team. They seized my trolley and raced me expertly through some shiny corridors. Suddenly Jeremy materialised, inexplicably wearing full surgical scrubs. Somehow I had been upgraded from 'Baby's pointing the wrong way; exercise caution' to 'Emergency Caesarean'. We burst through the swing doors of an operating theatre. My excitement at finding myself in a cameo role on *ER* was considerably dulled by the realisation that I was about to be carved up like a roast chicken.

I attempted to negotiate with the registrar. 'Listen, I would actually prefer to just give birth naturally,' I told her. 'What about if I give it a go and you folk just keep an eye on me and leap in if it seems to be going wrong? Would that work?' She actually rolled her eyes, and I became aware that an anaesthetist was plunging a needle into the back of my left hand. At the strikers' end, another mob-capped person murmured eight of the most alarming words in the English language: 'I'm just going to put a catheter in.' This was all escalating rather quickly.

Then, something remarkable happened. Catheter lady said, 'Hang on a minute. What's going on here? This baby isn't breech. I can see its head!'

An awful silence ensued, broken by my midwife, who in the tiniest of voices muttered, 'Oh my god. I'm so embarrassed.'

It turns out that my daughter, as a foetus, had amused herself in the womb by developing a head that looked amazingly like an arse. She was bald as a peanut, and her scalp had some sort of mad crease that looked like a bum crack. Which is why we were all here. No one could think of anything else to say. The air was full of latexy snapping sounds, which is what an elite medical team sounds like when they disgustedly peel off their gloves all at once. 'Well, there you go,' said the registrar, with what I thought was an unnecessary snarky tone. 'You can go off and have your baby any way you want now. And there won't be a doctor in sight. Happy?'

They all stormed out, leaving me, Jeremy and the midwife staring at each other. She grabbed a wheelchair. I hopped off the slab and settled into it. And off we went through the hospital looking for somewhere to have this baby. I became convinced I could hear the *Benny Hill* theme tune playing in the background.

The good news is that we found an unoccupied birthing suite. Weirdly, it even had a birth pool in it. So it all happened the way I had planned, and yes babies do swim about underwater when they're born, and yes it is super cool. And the National Health Service observed, in our case, its normal practice of discharging mothers and newborns after about five hours, so by nightfall we were back in our own flat, where I finished making the chutney.

The other part of the NHS post-natal care system, which is that midwives visit you at home to help you with feeding and so on, didn't happen in our case because no one could agree on who had actually delivered my child. Babies are like wickets – they have to be chalked up to someone. And my daughter had been delivered by a birth centre midwife, but in a different hospital. So she was nobody's responsibility.

By day three, the poor child was really losing condition as a result of her mother's well-meaning but deeply incompetent attempts at breastfeeding. The lovely olive skin we enthused about to our parents turned out to be quite severe jaundice. Audrey was a plucky child but it must have been hard, by this point, for her to reach any conclusion other than that she had been born to idiots. When I showed her to my GP, he took one look at her and said, 'You need to be in hospital.' So we raced to the University College Hospital – our fourth medical facility.

When we arrived, there was a media scrum outside. It turns out that the former Russian spy Alexander Litvinenko, who had fled the KGB, was in the very same hospital dying of radiation poisoning after some Putin patsy popped some polonium in his cup of tea. Litvinenko was electrifying the world by giving regular deathbed interviews in which he denounced the Russian state. Audrey and I settled into our room, which – in this overcrowded hospital – was not a room at all, but a waiting area that had been curtained off into four tiny tent-like enclosures. We shared ours with a fifteen-year-old girl and her newborn. Once a day her parents would visit, with faces like thunder. On one occasion the baby's father arrived. He looked, if anything, younger than her.

We entered a strange tangle of hospital bureaucracy. Every morning, a paediatrician would visit and exclaim on Audrey's good progress and express the opinion that we were just about ready to go home, and that tomorrow morning we could have our discharge form signed. But the next morning, it would be a new paediatrician who also felt that we were nearly good to go, and that tomorrow morning would be an ideal time to leave. Every day, a new paediatrician offering the same retreating horizon.

On Day Five of our stay, Litvinenko died. The hospital was in uproar. Cameras everywhere, everyone checking their beverages for polonium. The matter had escalated into the most serious diplomatic scandal since the Bulgarian defector Georgi Markov was murdered while walking over the Waterloo Bridge in 1978 by secret police, who shot a ricin pellet into his leg by means of a sharpened umbrella.

The chances of our receiving our discharge papers seemed slight. Jeremy and I felt as though we were trapped in our own Soviet bureaucratic tangle. Would we grow old in this tiny curtained room? We waited for night to fall, and then we just left. Packed up our things and our baby, strolled out of the hospital's entrance, past the media throng, hopped aboard the N5 bus, and went home. Nobody noticed. We were free. Tired, useless, and probably technically on the run from a range of health and child protection services, but free.

The Flaming Guitar

Steve Lucas

I NEVER ASPIRED TO be a musician. At age nineteen I didn't have anything much by way of aspirations at all. I could play a handful of open chords on an old classic guitar my uncle had bought me, and that was about it. I had written one song, 'Movin' On', about the loss of an imagined girlfriend, and co-written a turgid ballad with my school friend Ian Krahe, called 'The A Minor Blues'. The rest of my repertoire was a bluff. It is amazing how many songs you can fumble your way through with three or four chords. I had committed to memory maybe forty-odd songs within a few months of toil and struggle. I owed the achievement to a photocopied handbook of songs for buskers that seemed able to boil down the most complex songs to three basic chords and, I confess, I had a gift for remembering lyrics and melody. I referred to it as my 'phonogaphic' memory.

In 1977 I found myself the lead singer of a band called X. We were part of a growing punk scene in Sydney, kind of picking up where that hard-rocking, seminal punk powerhouse of a band Radio Birdman had left off. Our fans were fanatical, at times carving Xs into their flesh, at other times content to just smash everything in sight. We were banned from thirty-two pubs and venues in Sydney but still managed to get by. The Stagedoor Tavern, The Bondi Lifesaver and Civic Hotel didn't mind the chaos. Our crowds were the hardest drinkers in town, and the pubs took more than enough over the bar to cover the damage done. It gave me a great deal of pleasure to get up and blow a gasket while barking out cynical and satirical lyrics and generally trying to make myself heard over the musical barrage of bass, thundering of drums and the screaming guitar.

That first incarnation of X was, to me, the definitive X. It featured Ian Rilen on bass, Steve Cafiero on drums and my best friend, Ian Krahe, was the guitarist. We recorded a bunch of demo tapes in 1977 that ended up under someone's bed. The 'lost tapes' were finally unearthed and released as *X-Spurts* in 2011. We did another session at the Australian Film and Television School as part of a contra deal, and this session in a 'real' 24-track studio. It was eventually released as a seven-inch vinyl EP called *Hate City* in 2000.

What made X so popular? When you are in a band you never get to see or feel what the audience does. All you get to do is hear it. We had an ex-cop on drums, a former window dresser on bass and two rebellious high-school drop-outs as lead guitar and lead singer. Chemistry! Ian Rilen and Steve Cafiero had been in well-known bands for at least ten years before X came along. Ian Krahe and I were pretty green, relatively untried, but full of attitude.

My early musical career had been limited to school choirs. But at age fifteen, under the most inauspicious circumstances, I became the lead singer for a band of no-name misfits from Granville Boys High. I'd been yanked out of one of the most prestigious schools in Sydney – Fort Street Boys High – and dumped into possibly the worst high school in New South Wales at that time. I was left there to fester for a year. It felt like ten. My mother had remarried and given birth to two sons, to add to my sister and me, and it was decided we needed a bigger house. The only place that we could afford was in Merrylands, a dull, flat suburb somewhere in Sydney's outer west. I was uprooted, re-zoned and very angry.

Granville Boys High was like an open detention centre for delinquent boys. Fights involving bike chains in the 'playgrounds' were not uncommon. Teachers fought a losing battle against our well-defended and predetermined ignorance. Classrooms were battle zones. Teachers were targets. Granville was the first high school to have its students go on strike: we collectively refused to cut our hair to the regulation one inch above the collar. Fail to comply and you would be caned. If that didn't work, you were suspended. If you still refused to obey, expulsion was the end of it. Ironically, Fort Street got all the attention when the students there went on strike in sympathy.

I fell in with a bunch of guys who were into music and studied it as an elective. I used to sit in class tapping out rhythms to songs that were on constant rotation in my head, and one of the guys heard me and asked hopefully if I played drums. I said no, but I liked to sing. This was a good thing because, even though they happened to need a drummer, they also needed someone who could really sing, as opposed to simply going through the motions. I was asked to audition, and I suddenly found myself in the school band. I was christened J.C. after John C. Fogerty of Creedence Clearwater Revival, thanks to my similar profile, haircut and flannelette shirt. These guys were fourteen going on fifteen and were serious about music. Everyone had a nickname and symbol, though these days it would be considered a tag. Spuddy T. and Danny Hoot Freakly were real characters. They were studying sax, clarinet and piano but teaching themselves bass and guitar.

It wasn't long before a fellow named John Connelly offered me the chance to buy his guitar. He was trading up and was willing to sell his no-name semi-acoustic guitar for the princely sum of twelve dollars. It had a floating scratch plate, a single pick-up, and a volume knob and a tone knob. None of which mattered because I didn't have an amp. But it was a guitar. First up, I needed some cash. My stepfather got me a gig working part-time sweeping the floors at a timber mill. That was fine, but he kept introducing me to everyone as his son, John. My name was Stephen. I was confused at first but then decided he probably did have a son called John, since he had been married before, and maybe he hadn't got around to telling anyone at his work that he had divorced and remarried. Okay, I had an active imagination!

I saved my dollars and bought the guitar one sunny day in 1973. Sometime around then my stepfather disappeared. He went to work one day and didn't come back. We never saw him again. That left my mother to cope with two toddlers and two teenagers. They were tough times, and I found some comfort in my guitar. I'd sit on the roof of our home and play for hours on end. Sometimes I'd serenade my mother, trying to cheer her up. This was back in the time of no single mother's pensions, in fact, no government support at all.

One day, after seeing a photo of John Lennon's white piano, I decided I wanted my guitar to be pure white. I put some serious hours into planning how I might go about this transformation. I managed to acquire some thinners, turpentine and other highly flammable ingredients to strip the varnish. After some thought, I decided the laundry was the best place to perform the operation. It was a fibro box with a cement floor that was attached to the back end of the house, out in the backyard. It was fitted out with a door, one window, a double sink, a washing machine, and a gas hot-water system. It was perfect – private, relatively dust-free and conveniently childproof. Plus, there was running water to wash with. I laid a few old towels on the floor in preparation. I had thought of everything. Then with surgical precision, I selected the tools I would need: screwdrivers, scrapers and whatnot. Carefully, I removed anything that was attached to the guitar – screws, machine heads, the scratch plate, the pick-ups and other odd bits and pieces – and put them neatly into a box.

It was a fine summer's day. A cloudless blue sky arched over suburbia, giving me a sense of quiet, reflective protection. I enclosed myself in the laundry and began work. I brushed the thinners, coat after coat, over the varnish of the guitar. It was hot work with the window jammed shut and the door closed to keep out dust and grit and anyone who might interfere with my work in process. Coat after coat after coat, I applied. The varnish began to turn into a jelly-like, glutinous, viscous, sticky goo. It seemed to be attaching itself to me and my clothing like the Blob. My head started spinning. I was getting high from the fumes. The fumes …

I should have opened the door or window – just an inch would have helped. Instead, I fixed my focus on the task at hand. I was now liberally pouring thinners and turps all over the guitar to try to wash away the gooey scum that seemed to be covering everything.

Of course, it was inevitable. The fumes had nowhere to go and the pilot light for the gas hot water was primed to ignite. I worried away at the guitar, oblivious to the danger, when suddenly, without warning, there was a silent explosion. Sort of an inverted *whoomp!* Almost a non-sound. The atmosphere in the laundry instantly converted into a ball of flame. It blew me through the door, knocking it off its hinges, and hurled me out and down the steps and onto the grass of the backyard.

Panic is a private thing with me; I panic silently. My head cleared, and I ran back up the stairs to see everything in the laundry aflame. Black smoke hung in the air, covering the walls and fixtures. I was still panicking silently, but only just. I grabbed the garden hose. We had good water pressure, and for a moment I dared to hope. I turned the hose onto the laundry in a desperate effort to put out the fire. It was futile. That glutinous, viscous, sticky goo was like napalm. It floated on the streams of water and began to flow like lava down the laundry steps. I could see my guitar burning. I had to save it. I ran in, grabbed the head stock and flung it out into the yard. To my horror the flaming goopy goo shot off it in clumps like meteorites, hitting the back fence, and happily started burning like it was sitting down to the main course. I screamed, all notions of quiet panic gone, and gave my full attention to the fence, having decided the laundry was lost anyway. I got the fence under control with the hose, then turned my attention to the laundry and its contents. Water was not helping, what to do? Aha! Smother the flame!

I turned off the hose and with a hop, skip and a jump over the flames, I grabbed some towels from the washing machine and used them to smother the fiery rivulets streaming down the steps. I stomped on the towels, turning them over and over, mopping up the water and thinners as well as blanketing the fire itself. I kept at it until I had the fire totally put out. I was exhausted but there was no time to rest. I knew if my mother saw this, she would freak. I surveyed the damage. It was then that I realised I could smell something funny. Other than the clinging fumes and turpentine. I looked down and saw that all the hairs on my arms had been burnt off. A trip to the bathroom and the mirror revealed that my eyebrows had shriveled and my hair was singed and smoking. I hosed myself down outside and stood there, immune to the beauty of the day. I could hear a pounding in my ears. Apart from the door, any harm done appeared to be mostly cosmetic. Smoke damage. I took heart and began scrubbing the blackened walls and ceiling. After I had soaped and scrubbed for what felt like forever, I used the hose to wash away the sad grey suds. I packed the screw holes in the door jamb and reattached the door. I'd have to repaint it, but that could wait. I cleaned and primed the water system, and then turned my attention to the washing machine. For a moment I felt like a hero. Then I remembered my guitar.

It lay there on the grass, a mottled, smoldering ruin, in the middle of our sunny, green backyard. The charred neck and body were basking in the sun, catching some rays. My whole being centered on the carcass of my guitar. Fury and rage built up in me over all that had just happened. The fact my stepfather had disappeared, leaving me at age fifteen to be 'the man of the house'. Again! I felt anger at my mother for marrying two losers. Anger at the violence that plagued the school I was forced to attend. Anger at the school rules! I was angry with the whole goddamn world! I picked up a mattock, strode purposely to the hapless instrument and hacked and pounded and smashed it into a thousand or more splinters. Then I hit it some more. When I finally exhausted myself, numbly I gathered them up, all the shards, bits and pieces, and dropped them, without ceremony, into the bin.

I got teased when I went back to school. But my hair grew out and my eyebrows grew back. I still sang with the band. I started playing truant. Never one for doing homework, I now ceased altogether. Something had changed. There was a new defiance in my walk, a new attitude in my vocal delivery. A threatening bitterness that kind of scared and thrilled my band mates. Days faded in and out. We rehearsed and chased girls. We broadened our taste in music. As the year moved towards its inevitable end, word got out that we really did sound okay. Good enough, in fact, to be asked to perform at school for the sixth form's (year 12) farewell dinner. We accepted. It felt good. We lulled the teachers into a false sense of security with songs like 'Father and Son' by Cat Stevens and other gentle acoustic numbers. Then as the sixth form guys started to get restless, we launched into 'Aqualung' by Jethro Tull. Taking great satisfaction in sneering out lyrics about a dirty old man sitting on a park bench dressed in shabby clothes. Revelling in the description of his greasy fingers and snot running down his nose as he watched the little girls run. Before we could be stopped, we chugged into 'Locomotive Breath' from the same album. Ah, the pleasure to be found singing to your headmaster and teachers about winners and losers and just who has who by the balls. The headmaster was red in the face. Teachers were up in arms. The prefects and sixth formers were as one, laughing maniacally. We ploughed on, hastening to the end of the set before they shut us down completely. The last song of the night was Deep Purple's 'Smoke On the Water'. I could see myself with a flare gun burning down the school. I swear my eyes were blazing as we burned through that song. We took and held the night. Fuck the guitar! You can do so much more with a voice.

That year saw the end of the suburban dream. Things had all gone to hell at home. My mother had a breakdown. My father had disowned my sister and me. It fell to my grandfather to bail us out. He found a place for us in Ashfield, a comfortable kind of suburb in Sydney's inner west.

My uncle, in a very generous act of kindness and understanding, bought me a beautiful classic guitar. It wasn't the same, but I appreciated the thought. How do you play rock'n'roll on a nylon-string guitar? I was reinstalled at Fort Street Boys, but I was a year behind and had no interest in catching up. The damage was done. I got kicked out of high school by year 10 and was advised not to enroll in any other secondary school in the state of New South Wales. I got a job in a car yard detailing and washing the new and used vehicles. I lost contact with the gang from Granville but stayed in touch with my friends, the few I had, at Fort Street. Eventually most of them dropped out too. Was it my fault or influence? I can't say.

I left the city. Went up north to a town called Armidale. A sleepy little town with ten churches and ten pubs. It was home to a teachers college and university. The youth of the town by far outnumbered the old. It was relaxed and easy going. Kind of like the last stand of the hippy generation it had just missed out on being a part of. I carved bowls out of soapstone to use in bongs. I dropped acid, smoked pot and listened to records. I played my nylon-string guitar around campfires. I hitchhiked around, picking fruit and doing nothing much in particular. Life was a dream. No matter how sweet the dream, sooner or later you got to wake up – or be woken up.

What can I say? My wake-up call came in the form of a telegram. Destiny intervened and had chosen my closest friend, Ian Krahe, to deliver it.

'New band. Bring voice. Love Nia.'

I thought I was ready for anything. Little did I know …

Boo

Juanita Phillips

D O YOU BELIEVE in ghosts?

I never used to. Until I lived in a house on the northern beaches that was teeming with them.

Now, even if you don't believe in ghosts, please note this was in Sydney, so I know you're going to like or at lease be scared of the real estate side of it. Let me tell you about this house.

It was built by a famous architect called Keith Cottier, in the 1960s. It was typical of what was known as the Sydney School of architecture. Imagine three big modern cubes, running down the side of a steep hill, overlooking the water and surrounded by towering spotted gum trees. The three cubes were connected by a central staircase, with rooms running off each side, and the kitchen and living areas were down the bottom. Remember the staircase – it's important.

My ex-husband and I bought this house when we got married and I was expecting my first baby, Marcus. He's just turned fourteen, so that's how long ago it was.

The house was really run-down but it had huge rooms, and floor-to-ceiling windows that looked out onto the bush and the water. We painted the walls white and stained the floorboards very dark, almost black. The light just streamed in. It was like living in an art gallery.

As soon as we moved in we noticed that it was quite a noisy house, especially at night. The floorboards in the central staircase creaked a lot. We'd listen to them as we sat downstairs watching TV. It sounded exactly like somebody was walking down them. We figured it was just the timber expanding and shrinking, and didn't think any more of it. But other people were starting to be a little bit freaked out by our house.

The night that Marcus was born, my mother was on her own there. She'd come down from Brisbane to help me when the baby arrived. We were at the hospital, an hour's drive away in Randwick. She was staying in the guest room, which was one of the bedrooms running off the central staircase.

At 3 am she was woken by a man's footsteps walking down the staircase. They were slow and deliberate, and surprisingly loud – loud enough to wake her. She checked her watch – that's how she knew what the time was – and immediately thought, Mario's home from the hospital! She listened to the footsteps continue down the stairs towards the kitchen, and thought, I'll get up and have a cup of tea with him and see how Juanita and the baby are.

Anyone who knows my mother, Gaye, knows that you do not stand between her and a cup of tea, no matter what time of the day or night it is. But by the time she put on her dressing gown and slippers, and opened the door onto the staircase, the house was silent. And dark. There was no light coming from the kitchen. She realised there was no one there. The house was empty.

She didn't tell me about that night for a long time. But just a few weeks later, I had my own strange experience. My husband had driven into the city to work, and I was alone at home with the baby for the first time.

Marcus was about three weeks old, and I'd put him in his blue bouncinette in the nursery while I went to have a shower. The nursery was off the staircase, opposite the guest room where my mother had stayed. And you know what a bouncinette is, right? One of the old-fashioned crocheted ones on a metal frame, with the sling that you put between the baby's legs to secure them.

Anyway, as I stepped out of the shower, I heard the unmistakeable sound of a man's footsteps coming down the staircase. They were slow and deliberate and … loud. I could tell that whoever it was, they were wearing boots, like a workman's boots.

I knew immediately that there was an intruder in the house. In that instant, I believed with every fibre of my being, that I was going to be murdered. When you're a woman, you go your entire life with that possibility sitting quietly in the background. I remember feeling very calm, but overwhelmed with sadness, and thinking, so this is how my life ends. The footsteps continued down the stairs and stopped outside the bathroom.

Standing there in my towel with dripping wet hair, I made a decision that if I was going to die, I was not going to be found cowering in a corner. I wanted to see my killer. I threw open the door and stepped out onto the landing.

There was nobody there.

I took a second to absorb that, then flew up the stairs to the nursery where my son was. I looked in and got the shock of my life. The bouncinette was empty.

By now, I really thought I was going mad. I stared at the empty bouncinette and felt – it's hard to describe – I felt like I was living the reality of someone whose baby had been stolen. In the same way that just minutes earlier, I'd felt that I was living the experience of a woman who was about to be murdered. I walked over to the bouncinette and stared down at it. I was already grieving. My baby was gone. And then on an impulse, I lifted it up.

Marcus was lying underneath it, looking up at me. He was on his back with his arms by his sides, completely straight, as though somebody had just laid him there. To this day, I cannot explain it. There is no way a three-week old baby can get themselves out of a bouncinette.

Over the next few years, things like that kept happening. We went out on a rare date night and returned to find the babysitter distraught and terrified. She insisted somebody had been in the house because she'd heard them walking around. 'Don't ever ask me to babysit for you at night again,' she said. 'This place gives me the creeps.'

When Marcus was learning to talk, he woke up one night and called for his father. It was just after three o'clock. When Mario walked into the nursery, Marcus was sitting up in his bed, pointing to the corner. 'Dadda, who's that lady sitting over there?' he asked.

Over time, we became accustomed to the strange goings-on, especially the footsteps. They stopped bothering us. But then, one Christmas Eve, when my daughter was just a few months old, my Croatian mother-in-law, Marija (also known as Baba), came to stay the night. We put her in the guest room, off the central staircase.

The next morning, I heard her rattling around in the kitchen at six o'clock, and I went down to see why she was up so early. She said, 'I want you to take me to church as soon as you can. I've had a terrible experience. I need to go to Mass.'

Marija told me that around 3 am she was woken by the sound of two people rushing and clattering down the stairs. There was a sense of urgency and panic about their movements. She immediately thought that something was wrong with the baby, and that Mario and I were rushing to attend to her. She tried to get out of bed to help us but she couldn't move. She felt a huge weight on her chest, as if somebody were sitting on it. 'And I smelt damp earth,' she said, 'as if my nostrils were full of soil. I felt like I was suffocating.'

She was absolutely petrified. The next time she came to visit, she brought an enormous and very ugly crucifix, which she insisted on hanging in the living room to drive away any evil spirits. But she never again stayed the night.

Now, anyone who's had kids knows what a disaster that was – a grandmother who stays overnight occasionally is essential to a parent's mental health. So I figured that we actually needed to sort out the ghost problem and get Baba back in the babysitting loop. I rang the most sensible person I know – my friend Lisa, who at the time was a senior manager at the ABC. Technically, she was my boss. And I was about to have the weirdest conversation with a boss in my career.

'Look, I need your advice on something,' I said. 'You'll probably think I'm crazy, but I think we have ghosts in our house, and I don't know what to do.'

Lisa responded very matter-of-factly, as if I'd just asked her to sign my annual leave form. 'No problem,' she said. 'I lived in a haunted house myself a few years back. You need to ring the Enmore Spiritualist Church. Ask for Pat. She's great at getting rid of ghosts.'

Who would have thought that haunted houses were so common? And that there was a lady called Pat who could sort them out for you?

I rang the church and got through straightaway. Pat turned out to be the Reverend Patricia Cleary. She was the president and treasurer of a group of clairvoyants who met every week at a house in Enmore and spoke to dead people. Pat told me she was eighty-four and she'd been busting ghosts for thirty years. She didn't put it quite like that. She described ghosts as trapped souls who didn't realise their human bodies had died. They sensed something wasn't quite right, but they didn't know what it was. As a result, they were confused and angry, and that energy could cause disturbances of the sort we were experiencing. They needed to be gently persuaded by other spirits that it was time to move to the next level.

'Great,' I said. 'So, you have a seance here and give the ghosts their marching orders?'

'Not so fast,' said Pat. First, she had to ask me a couple of questions. Was anyone in the house suffering from mental illness? Or taking illicit drugs?

I was a bit taken aback by that. But Pat explained that about 90 per cent of the ghost reports received by the Spiritualist Church turned out to be psychotic episodes, not paranormal activity. Apart from wasting everybody's time, it was also a matter of personal safety. So the church clairvoyants no longer did house calls. The process was done remotely. And it wasn't called a seance, she said. It was called a circle, and during the circle, which was usually held on a Friday night, the church people would make contact with their helpful spirit guides, who would then be dispatched to help the trapped souls transition out of this plane to the next.

After I convinced Pat I wasn't mentally ill or on ice, I booked us in for the following Friday. Pat asked for our address, so she could pass it on to the spirit guides.

'We need the postcode too,' she said.

'Spirits need postcodes?' I asked.

'Of course!' said Pat. 'We don't want them going to the wrong suburb.'

I had an image of a couple of ghosts zooming up the Wakehurst Parkway, saying, 'Do we go right or left at the lights?'

There was one thing I was still curious about. Our house had been built in 1967. There seemed to be several trapped souls rattling around in it. As far as I knew, there hadn't been a mass murder there, at least not in the past forty years. So where had all these ghosts come from?

Pat said it was possible they were residents from previous dwellings that had been pulled down. Or they could be homeless people who'd camped on vacant land around Sydney during the Great Depression. Or this might go even further back, to the time of the white invasion. That was interesting, I thought, because not long before, while we were landscaping, we had discovered a lead cannonball buried deep in the earth. And we knew from researching local history that both Captain Cook and Arthur Phillip had sailed up this waterway.

Anyway, who knows? Maybe it was all a figment of our imagination. But what I can say is that after the Enmore psychics held their circle, we never heard the footsteps again.

I was so curious to find out what had happened, that over the following months, I tried to call the church numerous times. I tried at all times of the day and night. Nobody ever picked up. It was as if the Enmore Spiritualist Church and its band of psychics had just disappeared.

I later found out why. Not long after our ghosts were persuaded to move on, the church was embroiled in a shocking financial scandal. Reverend Pat was removed as treasurer and accused of embezzlement. There were allegations that bikies had infiltrated the church. People were literally locked out of the church. The matter went all the way to the Supreme Court, and eventually the church closed, ninety-eight years after it had opened.

All the psychics said they hadn't seen it coming!

In 2008, we sold the house and moved closer to the city. I was happy to leave it. Even though the ghosts had gone, I always felt a sadness about it. I've lived in two other houses since then and, I'm happy to say, neither of them has been haunted. But there's something about our old house that I can't quite let go. I still dream about it.

And every so often, I google the address. I've noticed that every couple of years it's up for sale again.

Nobody stays for long.

Bridget Jones's
Crime Scene

Rick Morton

THIS IS HOW I discovered my brother, Toby, was a drug addict.

He became an artist. He started calling himself Shroomy, and painting mushrooms on any available surface in psychedelic colours. He told me he wanted to sell them, which was great news for any interior designers who'd ever considered the wares at a weekend market and thought, no, not shit enough.

Psychosis, among other things, ensures the dramatic lowering of the bar for artistic merit, and my brother, Shroomy, was its newest wunderkind. The few people who bought them, he thought, were intelligent, free agents of the marketplace. But it turns out they were in psychosis, too, and psychosis had done to art criticism what it had also done to merit. I was torn between my instinct to support the creative streak in him and the knowledge that if he found out that there was a streak of anything, he would attempt to crystallise it and smoke it.

'He's drawn a fucking mushroom on my shoe. I'm not kidding, Rick. On my good work shoe. Who does that?' Mum told me once.

Toby was a meth addict, an ice junkie. He lived in his own fortress of squalitude underneath my mum's house, against her will.

Over the summer of 2016, Mum set about her usual festive handiwork, stitching reindeer to send to her children as Christmas decorations. At the same time, she discovered Toby was working on a little craft project of his own, blowing glass ice pipes around a drum under her Queenslander house. It reminded me of some of the more diverse episodes of *Better Homes and Gardens*, where the gardener builds an outdoor planter box while Noni Hazelhurst sets up a safe injecting room. Mum was both furious and what I would describe as angry-proud.

'How the hell did he learn glassblowing, Rick? That's what I want to know,' she said to me down the phone. There was a pause before she added resolutely, 'It's a skill!'

I love my brother, don't get me wrong, but his addiction to drugs had become dangerous for my mum. His friends would visit at all hours and in all states of dysfunction. Her home was like a Noah's Ark but for shit people.

During a third attempt to get a domestic violence order placed against him, Mum went directly to the local country coppers, and they explained they were powerless to help unless he was literally in the act of trying to kill her.

'I'll kill him myself,' Mum said in frustration.

'Debbie, I don't need to hear that,' the police officer said.

By way of defence, and I stress this is not and should never be used as a defence, Mum helpfully furnished the law man with some more detail. 'I don't have a gun, I don't have a knife,' she said, as if this was some kind of masterclass in poverty. Again, Mum had been foiled not by motivation or effort but by a lack of access to resources.

Toby continued living under the house and his friends essentially moved in. Take Scotty, a career criminal who has plied his trade in the small country town we call home since he was in primary school. He was the first man who ever robbed us. Now, it's just my opinion, but if you're going to be a career criminal you should probably do it in a place where there are at least three other criminals, just to give yourself a chance. Like all good regional towns, ours had the butcher, the baker, the candlestick maker, and Scotty, the bicycle taker.

Scotty was fingered so many times for his crimes that he has spent about half his short life in prison, where he has also been fingered.

In July last year I was back home visiting Mum and we had embarked on that great version of bonding that mothers and their gay sons get into: watching *Bridget Jones's Baby*. Before I came out, it used to be *Priscilla Queen of the Desert*, and Mum would always drop hints about how wonderful the drag queens were. I was terrified of being gay and fairly sour on buses, so I always found those sessions a little underwhelming.

Halfway into the movie there was a loud commotion underneath the house and Mum went running down the stairs to investigate, which alarmed me. Although she is very short and as such has a very low centre of gravity, I am always worried about her getting hurt.

'Fatboy, go home,' she yelled.

My brother had many friends with bad nicknames. Fatboy is an obvious one but then there is Beetle, who I like to think was named so because he once rolled onto his back and couldn't get up. Fatboy ran off, quick as a flash, and all seemed right with the world until Scotty emerged from under the house, clutching his neck, just below the jaw.

'Toby, I've been stabbed!' Fatboy had broken a golf club in half and plunged the severed metal shaft into Scotty's neck.

He fell to his knees on the pavement and lay down, blood pooling under his head. 'I can't feel my face!' A face is something you want to be able to feel at all times. Mum phoned the police while I phoned the ambulance.

My brother's dog, Ziggy, was part pig mutt and part kangaroo, with a brain that seemed to have been switched off not long after she was born. She proceeded to spring through the blood and over Scotty while Toby left his bleeding friend and went to the fence to reassure some passers-by that everything was in order, which of course it wasn't.

The cockatiel was screeching, our dog Jack was barking, Ziggy was getting bloodier by the second and Mum's cat, Charlie, had eyes the size of dinner plates. Scotty, of course, was crying out into the night. This is why the Comancheros and the Rebels never do business at the zoo.

Toby decided to drive his friend to the local hospital instead of waiting for the ambulance. It didn't occur to me that he would just dump him there. But at that point, as I was chaining the spring-loaded turbo dog to the Hills Hoist, I wouldn't have been surprised if a herd of naked chickens turned up demanding the return of their feathers from my pillow.

Toby was back in five minutes to clear out anything incriminating under the house and do a runner. He had a little backpack and looked a lot like Dora the Explorer, if Dora had done time for grievous bodily harm and subsequently binged on methamphetamines.

'Why'd you have to call the cops for? They make everything worse,' my brother yelled at me. Now, I realise this is a matter of perspective. If you are the one-time victim of police brutality who is getting married and has planned a strictly enforced fireman-themed strip-show only to have the hot cops turn up, my bad, that's on me. If your fucken mate stabbed your other fucken mate in the fucken neck, I'm going to call the lawboys because I get incredibly turned on by the mere hint of public order and safety.

The local police sergeant turned up. 'Oh, g'day, Rick, I haven't seen you in years,' he said cheerfully through the screen door. He asked me to take him in detail through everything that happened.

'Well, Mum and I were watching *Bridget Jones's Baby*,' I told him.

'So, watching a movie upstairs?'

'*Bridget Jones's Baby*,' I reminded him.

'Yeah, we probably don't need that level of detail,' he said

Oh, so we're just going to give up on Renée Zellweger's happiness now? Is that how this night is going to go? It just gets better.

During the statement, Mum's cat knocked something over in another room and Mum yelled out, 'What's Charlie into? Drugs, probably!'

The detectives left our home at 1 am. There were crime scene chemicals and dust all over the place downstairs and the house was quiet. I looked at Mum.

'Do you … want to just finish the movie?'

'Of course, darling,' she said. 'You would not believe the shenanigans our Bridget gets up to. Oh, and someone drove past and threw two Molotov cocktails at the house, but I really have no idea what that was about.'

Scotty escaped from the hospital two days later – there was no television, he said – and I found him that morning, sitting in the garden with his hospital wristband still attached. Half his face was drooping on account of nerve damage the doctors thought might be permanent. Actually, his face looked like a landslide. Despite the fact he could have died, Scotty was more worried about the new girl he had met who wanted to 'jump his bones'.

And that's how we found ourselves there in the morning sun: a recidivist criminal with a bung face asking a gay man how he was going to go down on his new girlfriend. They say we humans tend to take stock and reassess our lives after a near-death experience, but Scotty? Scotty was horny.

Got Lost on the Way, Baby?

Sally Rugg

D O YOU EVER get lost in your own house?

It's a very peculiar experience. You walk into your living room and the doorways have moved around the walls. Where the door to your kitchen used to be is now a solid blank wall. There's a quick, irrational moment when you wonder if you've woken up in a stranger's house, but those are definitely your things everywhere – it's just that the structure of your house has shifted. The architecture got bored in the middle of the night and rearranged itself. Moving your eyes along the solid wall, a doorframe skitters into your vision on a wall your brain is insisting did not have a door in it last night. Then suddenly the house seems to reassemble itself. So, if the kitchen's there, then the bathroom is in front of you, not behind you. Right?

Do you ever feel the world spin when you're walking in a straight line?

You know that from your house, the train station is a seventeen-minute walk and has one right turn. You know that if you just keep walking straight until you're at the train line, at which point you turn right, then you'll be at the station in seventeen minutes. Easy. Just keep walking straight ahead along the footpath.

You've walked for five minutes and start to feel uneasy; you're going the wrong way. Nothing looks familiar. You must have turned around and gone back the way you've come from; you do that sometimes. Every step forward feels like a pull backwards. You've gone the wrong way. Christ, you're in a completely different neighbourhood now. How many minutes has it been? You must have turned down that street near the top of the hill where you always get confused, because you can't see the street ahead, and now you've marched off into the next suburb. None of these houses is familiar. Your heart starts to beat faster and the familiar panic of being lost starts to flutter through your body: 'Where am I?'

You pull out your phone and open your map. There you are, a little blue dot on the same street you walk along every day from your house to the train station. You walk a little further, to see whether you're still going the right way, and you are! False alarm. You're okay. You keep the map out as you continue to walk in a straight line. You will continue to use the app for the rest of the week until you have the confidence to try walking down a straight road unassisted once more.

Statistically speaking, my brain is probably not like yours. There is a very good chance that your hippocampus and your prefrontal cortex work together and give you the ability to form cognitive maps that allow you to conceptualise the space around you beyond your line of vision. Congratulations, genius. My brain, however, grew in utero with a fun little quirk called Developmental Topographical Disorder (DTD), which means that I'm going to take a few more minutes than you would to get back from the bathroom in this restaurant unless you come with me, please.

Having DTD isn't like having a poor sense of direction or not being very good at reading maps. It's a permanent disorientation that renders you completely lost beyond what you can see in your immediate surroundings. Often, it's an absolute catastrophe.

A few months before Alan Jones ordered the Premier of New South Wales to force the CEO of the Sydney Opera House to allow gambling advertisements to be projected on its sails, I gave a talk there. It was meant to be an inspiring seminar on how to be an activist, and because it was an hour long, I couldn't just get up on stage and shout, 'Don't ever let anyone tell you what to do!' like I'd hoped to.

I'm a young, female activist who speaks in the public domain, which means I receive a lot of violent threats from angry men on the internet, who perceive any discussion of justice or opportunity for minorities as a personal attack on their privilege. Which I suppose it is, really. In the lead-up to this talk, I'd received some quite specific threats from one particularly angry internet stranger, so the Opera House staff were taking a little extra care with security. I was brought to my own green room through a secret underground door and up through a labyrinth of backstage passageways and a dozen identical, winding corridors. Needless to say, I had absolutely no idea where I was beyond 'Opera House'.

Thankfully, a lovely runner took me down to the stage with plenty of time to spare. As established, the seminar was slightly more complex than me pounding my fist on a lectern repeating, 'Always ignore politicians who tell you things aren't possible', so I was nervous. So nervous that I needed a little wee before going onstage, as I assume all professionals do.

'No worries, if you just head back the way we came and then at the end of the hall take a left and follow that around the corner, you'll see it on your right', my friendly runner told me, hurrying off to their next job, leaving me standing there looking gormless as they trotted off into the horizon.

I was sure I'd botch it. I weaved my way through backstage hallways with a knot in my stomach, certain I'd get lost coming back and that I'd be late for my big talk, or as much of my big talk I could get through before being potentially attacked on stage by a middle-aged man who felt angry about my wildly original belief that misogyny is bad. I had my phone out in front of me, clicking it on every ten seconds or so to check how late I was and how to balance rushing back to the stage for my big Opera House debut with getting myself even more lost.

I did manage to find my way back to the stage, only alarming the stage manager and sound technician for the ten minutes it took me to stumble, disoriented and alone, back from the bathroom. Furthermore, the security detail at the back of the theatre did not have to intercept a single angry stranger. All in all, it was a roaring success.

The day my sister gave birth to my niece, however, didn't run so smoothly. Not for her and certainly not for me. Bessie had a high-risk pregnancy, so my mum, my other sister and I joined her at the hospital for the big birthing showdown. It was fairly fraught and a little bit scary, so we were doing what all good family members do when their loved one is faced with their potentially imminent death – we blew up rubber gloves and pretended to write silly notes on her chart. It was the very least we could do.

Hospitals are funny places, aren't they? So many doors. So many of those trolleys that all look the same. So many moving curtains, changing what you remembered the room to look like.

A couple of hours into the labour, my sister's unborn baby stopped moving. The baby's heart rate dropped right down and doctors from across the hospital floor rushed to her room with their pagers beeping. It felt like hours had gone by, but maybe it was only minutes. Every second that baby didn't move felt like an age was passing, and nothing Bessie did made a difference, no matter where or how she moved. My darling sister turned to me, her eyes full of fear, and begged me to get her a lemonade from the vending machine. She was certain that the fizz and the chill and the sugar hit would stir the baby up again and re-engage her for her big entry to the world.

Lemonade. Vending machine. By the lifts. Got it.

An extra cool thing about my disorientation disorder is that when I'm flustered or stressed, it gets far worse. It's much like trying to do anything that requires careful deliberation and attention to detail when you're in an absolute flap. Computers fail you. Your six-digit pin won't reset. You've burnt the garlic and the smoke detector won't stop. You're trying to parallel park and you're blocking a massive queue of cars while also being late for the play you've paid a fortune to go to see. When stressed, the task of navigating myself from A to B is rigged against me, every step trying to trip me up and every corner a trap.

I was frantic. My unborn niece's life potentially depended on this lemonade. I'd done nothing to help my poor sister as she howled and heaved in agony other than put the bedpan on my head and say, 'Look at my funny hat!' She'd asked this of me in her moment of need. There was no way I would let her or the baby down. All I needed to do was find the vending machine and make my way back to her room.

I ran Lara Croft-style through the hospital, swerving past nurses and dodging patients on drips. Straight ahead, left, right, right again, my Birkenstocks flip-flopping on the squeaky-clean floor. As I burst through the ward's double doors, I saw it, the vending machine. The lemonade. I fumbled with the coins I'd snatched from the bottom of my mum's bag, wildly feeding them into the slot. The can dropped to the bottom of the machine with a thud and I took off back to the room.

The double doors swung in my wake as I sprinted down the corridor. One door, two doors, three doors. Left. Keep going, past the linen room, a little bit further … and then it's right, right? Right. Yes. Or was it left? My sprint had dropped to a jog, faltered to a walk, and finally I stopped dead in my tracks. I didn't know where to go. I was clutching the lifesaving lemonade – for all I knew my niece had moments to live – and I was a terrified deer in the fluorescent lights of the maternity ward. Possibly the maternity ward. A ward. I had absolutely no idea where I was beyond 'Hospital'.

I didn't know where to go and nothing looked familiar, so I just started running. If I ran around the whole wing, I'd be sure to find the room. 'I will recognise the room,' I told myself as tears streaked down my face. I'll be there within seconds and then the baby will be okay, and my sister will be okay. I ran and I ran. Nothing looked familiar. I was going back the way I came. I didn't know where I was going. This was my nightmare.

It felt like minutes, but it would have been seconds later that I saw the room, down the end of the corridor. I remembered how the curtain was drawn, the writing on the whiteboard by the door, the cleaning trolley out the front. With a fresh surge of urgency, I tore down the hallway with the lemonade in my sweaty hands, each stride bringing me closer to saving a life. I ran straight through the doorway exclaiming, 'It's here, it's here!'

Flinging the curtain to the side, I busted open the lemonade. As the fizzy drink exploded all over me, all over the floor and all over the feet of a total stranger – who on reflection I'd say was about eight centimetres dilated – I realised I was in the wrong room.

'I'm so sorry!' I shrieked, as the poor woman bellowed, 'Get out!', kicking with one of her legs, either to shake off the lemonade or in completely understandable self-defence against the sticky, crying woman who had just burst into her room. Mortified, I yanked the curtain closed and nearly smacked a nurse in the face, who'd assumedly been responding to the misleading cries of, 'It's here! It's here!', which when shouted in a maternity ward probably rarely means, 'Your Schweppes has arrived.'

'I'm so sorry!' I shouted again, running from the room covered in tears and fizzy drink.

'Sally! Over here!'

I spun around to see my mum standing a few doors down and beckoning me over. She looked confused as I ran towards her.

'Why are you running?' she asked with a slightly scornful head shake.

'The baby! It needs the lemonade!' I panted back.

My mum paused to take in the full spectacle of her sticky, weeping, panting first-born daughter, probably concerned that I might think an unborn baby might need or, indeed, be able to drink from a can while in utero.

'The baby is fine. We're at a hospital – the doctors know how to deal with this sort of thing,' she said, tutting at the state of me. 'She's about to push now so we're going to go and sit in the waiting room.'

Twenty minutes later, baby Penny joined the world and made me the proudest, stickiest aunty of all time.

Tolkien suggested that not all those who wander are lost. I suppose that's true. Some people enjoy hiking in the wilderness or exploring foreign cities or shopping at a Westfield. I wonder sometimes what it's like to wander. To understand how the space around you spreads and unfurls so that you can move through it however you please. For me, though, I will stick to the beaten track and the road most travelled and save getting lost for when I look into Penny's big, blue eyes – and the dozen other times each and every day.

Debra Racks Off to Melbourne

Richard Glover

WHO'D LIVE ALONE? I know millions do it. Just not me. Not until now. Suddenly my partner Debra is perpetually in Melbourne. I imagine she's shacked up with either a crime lord or a wanky theatre director – those two occupations being my only available image of what people do in Melbourne.

She likes Melbourne. I'm not so sure about the place. It's certainly a different sort of town to Sydney. In Melbourne, the phrase 'a splash of colour' means a whip-thin girl with pink-hair and a little black dress; in Sydney it means a footballer vomiting onto the Corso.

So it's me, the dog, and occasionally one son, and what can only be described as a downward trajectory – downwards to the full catastrophe. Here's my question for those who live on their own. How do you maintain standards? If no one is there to witness that second bowl of ice-cream, or the fifth glass of wine, then has it really happened? Is it like the tree that falls unobserved in the forest?

This is the way I find myself behaving as a single person: a man with no standards, no self-respect, and – crucially – no witnesses.

Most of my good behaviour, I now realise, is an attempt to impress Debra and distract her from the less savoury aspects of my character. This is all very well, right up to the moment she goes away. Robbed of the chance to brag to your partner – 'See, I did all the laundry'; 'The bathroom, you might notice, is spotless'; 'My fungal infection is clearing up' – how do you manage to maintain an interest in such matters? What's to stop the laundry from piling up, together with the household garbage and the unwashed plates and pans, until the neighbours start complaining about the stench, the council whacks a fumigation order on the house and you find yourself the subject of a tabloid current affairs show? 'Strange Hermit Lives with Rats and Mice in Fetid House of Shame' is presumably the headline they will use to advertise my story.

Certainly, with every night alone, my behaviour worsens. Debra generally flies to Melbourne on a Monday morning, and stays a week or sometimes two. The first Monday night, I'm fine. Home-cooked dinner, two beers, a news show on TV, one chapter of a literary novel and bed. By Tuesday, it's a frozen dinner, five wines, a comedy DVD and a perve at the catalogue for the DJs lingerie sale. Plot this on a chart and you'll see the steepness of the curve. By Friday, I'm pissed by 8.30 pm, no dinner, the dog's whining for food, I'm lying on the couch watching the arse-end of my ten-DVD Steve Coogan box-set, finding myself unable to comprehend the simplest of Steve's plots. By this point, I've lost the gift of language and am communicating with the dog via a series of grunts and whistles.

Continue this for a few weeks and I doubt I'd be fully human. Evolution itself would be thrown into reverse. Week two and the opposable thumb would go; week three and I'd lose the ability to walk erect. Stay away long enough and I'd probably become aquatic.

The supermarket doesn't help. I go shopping on Sunday afternoon to stock up for the week, and that's when the downward spiral begins. I search for things in packets for one, but the choice is extremely limited. Some packets explicitly say: 'Serves two.' It's the first time in my life I've been openly mocked by packaged meat.

Oh, I know it's possible to buy the two-pack and freeze half, but why should I? It's like a letter of reproach, sitting there in the fridge, the packaged meat mumbling the message, 'Hey, buddy, I happen to notice you are living on your own.'

And, so, I settle for a pack of smoked salmon, some pasta and a tub of cream; I'll get three dinners out of it. Sure, it's fattening, but who cares? If a man gets fat in the forest – with nobody there to witness the outward slump of his belly – has the weight gain really occurred? If he eats takeaway pizza straight from the box, observed only by the dog, is the universe any the wiser?

Half the people I know live alone. They seem perfectly happy. Their houses are tidy; their waistlines reasonable. Their alcoholism seems no more advanced than my own. How do they do it? Can it be that they develop some sort of internal system of standards and hygiene, rather than simply forcing their partner into the role of police officer, diet coach and moral arbiter?

Self-regulation. I turn the concept over in my mind and find it quite remarkable. Thing is, these days you are meant to cope. In fact, you're not even allowed to mention that it might be a bit of a challenge.

'Melbourne? Lovely. Two weeks? Super. I'll hardly notice you've gone.' This, I think, goes for both men and women. Since housework and childcare are such contested areas, you can never admit that any task normally done by your partner was anything but a delight when it becomes your turn to do it.

'Getting the children to sport on time? Oh, that was no trouble at all. And isn't it pleasant having that hour walking around the park in the bracing, freezing air while you wait for them to finish?'

During the second week, the mess is really building. By Monday, the kitchen floor already features eight dead cockroaches plus a moat of dropped food. By Tuesday, there are fifteen dead cockroaches, who appear to have organised their bodies across the floor to spell out the words: 'Sweep me'.

Debra, I notice, dropped large amounts of laundry into the basket just before her departure. She also did 'a clean-out' of the fridge – throwing out any food past its use-by date. This, of course, is precisely the sort of food that can sustain a family through a crisis. I conclude she has a plan to make the house fall apart during my stewardship, thus proving her contention that she does all the housework and I do nothing. I resolve to defeat her.

To save time, I cook all the family's meals in one go: an army-sized quantity of bolognaise sauce, sufficient to last five consecutive meals. The recipe contains one glass of red wine, the rest of the bottle going into the chef.

By Wednesday, my head is pounding due to the constant alcohol abuse. There are now twenty-two dead cockroaches, their bodies arranged to spell out the phrase: 'He's losing it'. This is when Debra phones in, wondering how we're all getting on.

Before answering, I remind myself: if you admit you're not coping, it's just another way of confessing that she normally does more than her share of this stuff. 'Fine,' I say. 'Absolute breeze. Getting a lot of reading in, actually. Great to be able to cook every night. A real pleasure.'

The only problem with this barefaced lie is the chaos that surrounds me. The dishwasher has chosen to break down. And most of the light bulbs in the kitchen have stopped working. I suspect Debra of sabotage. I have an image of her working behind enemy lines in World War Two Germany, but I say nothing.

The phone call ends, and I set to work. In the days ahead, the illusion must be created that we coped effortlessly. I square my shoulders. I have three days before her return to Sydney. I tackle the ironing and clean the bathroom, which is more disgusting than can easily be explained. The kitchen, though, appears to be fighting back against my attempts to clean it. Spaghetti sauce is evident on most surfaces, and fifty-seven deceased cockroaches now litter the floor, their bodies spelling out the words: 'She's winning'.

My son has turned up for dinner and is sullenly spooning down the bolognaise sauce that I've given him the last ten times he's visited. He says he feels sick and leaves the table. I keep eating, which is hard when you are overhearing the sound of your son vomiting into the rose garden.

Back in the kitchen, the cockroaches have reorganised themselves into a giant clock-face, counting down the minutes until Debra's return. With the cockroach clock ticking, I work through the night, scrubbing and cleaning. I remove all signs of the town of Bologna and its famous sauce. I try to fix the dishwasher and install new light bulbs. I run up to the shops to buy fresh milk and bread. Panting slightly, I arrive home with seconds to spare.

'The place looks great,' says Debra, breezily, as she walks in.

'Oh, does it?' I say, glancing up from the newspaper. 'I hadn't noticed.'

The scene is perfect save for my son, who is lying by the back door holding his stomach and groaning. Looking quite red in the face, he keeps mouthing the words, 'The bolognaise.'

'Is he all right?' Debra asks.

'Oh, yeah,' I say. 'He probably just ate too much of my cooking. It was delicious.'

She looks worried, but I'm not too concerned. We're alive. The house has not burnt down. There have been no major outbreaks of disease.

The full catastrophe? Well, on this occasion, I think it was averted. Frankly, I hardly noticed she was gone.

Burpin' Your Bad Voodoo ...

Sarah Macdonald

MY FULL CATASTROPHE is a story of dogs, death, disease, pestilence, infestation, elimination, evisceration and blocked auras. It's actually the story that started this whole catastrophic idea.

It was May 2015 and life was going okay. It was the first time in a decade I felt *almost* under control. I was emerging from that vortex of having really young kids and an often-travelling husband. I'd started a new job, he was travelling less, and my kids were taking faltering steps to independence. Our daughter had started high school and was managing reasonably well and our son was in that lovely year 4 stage of no homework, great fun and good friends. Even the dog seemed relatively content.

And then my dad died.

My dad was my rock and my family's anchor. He was a beautiful, calm, gentle man. My grief was huge and vast and only somehow made bearable by the fact it was uncomplicated. My grief was pure. I had always felt deeply loved by my father. In fact, the only competition my mum, siblings and I ever felt for Dad's love was his adoration for his dogs. Dad loved his dogs. He loved how they loved absolutely and unconditionally. As a lifelong atheist he used to point out that 'God' was 'Dog' backwards.

Dad loved all dogs and he even tolerated it when I got a non-allergic, stupid, fluffy, delicate, neurotic cavoodle and called him Shaggy. I did once hear Dad whisper to his big, jowly boxer dog, 'Shaggy's not a real dog but be nice to him, he can't help being pathetic.' Dad was right, Shaggy was pathetic. But he was sweet. And I needed him after Dad died for his constant companionship.

But grief that's pure is still grief. And after witnessing an awful end to my dad's beautiful life, I was traumatised. I collapsed into a black hole of despair, awaking from nightmares as a vulnerable and exposed and raw shell of a human being. I was in no shape for anything to go wrong.

So, of course, everything went wrong.

First, my bloke went overseas to study for two months. We'd already paid for it, we couldn't cancel, I told him to go. I was used to single parenting. We'd be fine.

My poor grieving mother then had a minor catastrophe. Mum can only handle life between 20 and 22 degrees. It was mid-winter and her heating system broke on the only non-globally warmed day of the year. Grief-stricken, vulnerable and freezing, she tried not to complain, but I spent days begging maintenance men to come. They finally came on her birthday and as they were fixing it, she asked me to check her back.

'It hurts a bit, what do you think it is?' she said.

My darling mum had big, red-raw, painful, pulsating shingles all over her back. Triggered by her grief, they showed how vulnerable she had become since losing her beautiful husband.

I bought her the drugs and put her to bed. The heating system got fixed. It lasted six hours. Guess what time it broke? Why of course, it broke on Friday at 5.01 pm. The temperature dropped. Her old house was as cold as a tomb. Her pain got worse. I spent the weekend screaming at the heating men's answering machines and voicemails. She got worse. The pain medication helped a bit but gave her horrendous nausea that was unmanageable. I was due to have a lovely afternoon tea with my girlfriends, with scones and champagne. Instead I took Mum to hospital and she spent four days behind a rainbow-striped curtain in a ward, mainlining apple juice and painkillers. I spent the days with my poor Mumma and my nights with the kids and my neurotic dog.

It was fine. It was life.

Mum came out of hospital and I went back to my new job just long enough to get the flu shot.

Then I got the fucking flu. And you know when you are really sick and you are really sad, and really lonely, and you are overwhelmed and overloaded and you go to the doctor and you just cry. I did that. The lovely doctor put on a mask, patted me on the back and gave me some flu medicine. She also gave me some Valium. She said to come back in a few days as I may need an X-ray for pneumonia.

I staggered home and lay for days with a fever. It was school holidays and I was crying with self-pity and pain, and downstairs my kids were crying with boredom. To this day I'm not sure what they did, but they survived. Rebecca Huntley, my partner in the titillating tome of terror that is this book, dropped off food but I didn't want anyone coming too close, so I stayed in isolation. My only companion and nurse was my dog, neurotic old Shaggy. But Shags is not a great nurse. In fact, he was so upset that I was so sick that he kept vomiting. So every time I'd stagger out of bed, I'd step in his vomit. It was revolting, but I needed him, so I let him lie on my bed. I thought I'd train him to sleep on the floor like a real dog when I was better.

My fever climbed to the point that I began to hallucinate. My thoughts became distorted, dreams became nightmares, and nightmares became real. In that state of altered consciousness everything suddenly became clear to me. I was not sick with a virus. I was possessed by bad voodoo! Those drugs were all well and good, but they weren't working because my issue was spiritual. So I did what all self-respecting daughters of an atheist would do. I messaged my most woo hoo of friends, Min, got the number of a dealer in dharma and rang a psychic. This lovely lady answered straight away and said, 'G'day, love, can't talk much now, I'm in Westfield.' Fair enough, I thought, spiritualists have to shop. Appraising my illness, isolation and state of sick sadness she took immediate charge. 'I'm gunna call you back, but I tell you what you're gunna do in the meantime. I need you to change your bed sheets to all white. I want clean white pillows and sheets and a white doona. Then I need you to get into a white bath of white salt water. Then get out of that bath and dress in white.'

'You betcha,' I told my new guru. Frankly, I would have done anything she'd said at that point. I'd broken the thermometer and I think my fever was off the scale.

I staggered around, changing my sheets to my good 1000-weave white cotton. I put on a new white doona cover. I had a bath with sea salt. I washed my hair. I put on my only white clothes – they were my nicest clothes.

The psychic rang me back and immediately burped loudly into the phone. 'Yep, *bbbbuuuuurrrpppph,* your aura, *burrrrrrpppphhhh,* is really blocked.' *Burrrrpppphhh.*

'Yes,' I said, 'it feels it, but would you like me to ring back when your indigestion is better?'

'No, darling,' she yelled. 'I'm cleansing your aura and I'm burping out your bad voodoo.'

'Of course,' I said, and on we went.

My saving-grace guru told me to imagine white light coming into the top of my head and down my body. And as I did so, she belched and burped, and she washed that bad voodoo right out of my hair. The dog did not like the loud belching – so loud he could hear it through the phone. He started to growl softly.

'Go with it, Shags, it's our only hope,' I said.

And, believe it or not, I actually could feel my aura getting clean. I felt white light enter my body through my scalp. And over a few minutes I could feel the top of my head grow warm. Then warmer. Then hot. Then hotter. Then I felt an amazing sense of itchiness as the bad voodoo left my body through the crown of my head.

I thanked my burping psychic and I hung up, immensely grateful.

But my head continued to feel hot. Until it got really itchy. And as I scratched the white-light laden scalp, it started to feel increasingly lumpy.

It was time to go back to the doctor. I arrived in my white best clothes, knowing that I was now cured, my lungs were clear and I would not need an X-ray for pneumonia. And I was right. She said my chest was clearing and my temperature finally falling.

This psychic is good, I thought.

As I turned to leave, I stopped, turned back and told my lovely, normal, sensible doctor about the really bad itchy pain I had on my head. I even told her about the spiritualist cleansing my aura. She looked at me with an expression that clearly signified she thought perhaps she'd given me too much Valium.

'Do you think perhaps it's like a saint, like a stigmata?' I asked her.

She looked at my head. 'No,' she said, 'it's not stigmata. You have nits.'

I walked out with a shame so burning it broke the new thermometer. I went home and deloused the kids' hair. And they both had long hair. I had long hair. And getting rid of nits is a shit of a job that involves a lot of poison and endless, strand-by-strand combing.

I was lonely, I was sad, I was sick, and I was so over it. I sat at the table with a big glass of Dettol for the comb and a big glass of wine for the comber. Every time I cleansed the comb, I'd take a drink from the wine glass. At some point late in the night, when I had become so incapacitated by exhaustion and fever, I drank the Dettol by mistake.

Right, I thought, this is it, I have had enough. My spirituality had almost faded away but in one last burst I said, 'Dad, I need you to send me a sign that everything is going to be all right, that my life is going to get better.'

No sooner had I spoken than the dog started yowling and crying.

Now this spooked me immensely, until I remembered that the poor dog hadn't had a walk for days as I was so sick and could hardly stagger. We live on the edge of a tiny patch of bush, so I let him out into the night. And I kept de-nitting my hair, all the time thinking about how, when I finished, I'd crawl into my lovely, clean, white, high thread-count sheets and go to sleep. I finished my hair. I put on about seven loads of washing with the towels and the kids' sheets and pillowcases. The dog came back and I let him in without a glance.

Shaggy trotted upstairs and the kids went to bed all shiny and new and clean. I finished the bottle of wine and the bottle of Dettol, put on the last load of washing, and then I started up the stairs. I was so tired I couldn't even stagger anymore. I crawled up those stairs to my nice clean sheets, thinking about how sometimes life is hard but I will get through this. I kissed the kids, and then headed to my bedroom, ready to sink into my white fluffy cloud of cleansed auras.

But as I approached my room my swollen, mucus-filled nose began to sense a smell. A revolting smell. An odious odour that made me gag. As I rounded the doorway, I saw the dog lying spread-eagled on my bed, with his head on my pillow. And as he put his head up to greet me, I noticed he had a big, long, brown smear of bloody, gross, skanky crap on his neck. It looked, smelled and had the consistency of liquid poo expelled from a dying animal, and it was mixed with offal, and there may even have been a bit of possum intestine hanging from his ear. This disgusting cocktail of crap was all over my dog and my best clean, white sheets and doona and pillow slips. And as I picked Shaggy up, I got it all over my nice white best clothes.

I began to laugh. Hysterically. In my room, alone, lonely, sad, stricken with grief and viruses and covered in crap, I put my head back and in a voice that was a mix of laughter, screaming, crying, hiccuping and banshee, I said, 'Thanks, Dad. You've shown me that life is sometimes offal and shit and you just have to roll with it and in it.'

And that, my friends, is how we began *The Full Catastrophe*. It's all about realising and learning that sometimes you just have to roll in the deep, deep doo-doo of life.

Part 2

Career Crises

Anatomy of a Stitch-up

Jenny Valentish

I T WAS HARD to pick a catastrophe since I actually have a tattoo on my back bearing the words 'Calamity Jen', but I'm going to take you back to 1992. I was seventeen and the CEO of *Slapper*.

This was my self-published magazine, full title – *Slapper: the groupie's guide to gropable bands* – or a 'fanzine', as the kids called them then. It would be a Tumblr now. *Slapper* was like an early ode to Rhonda Byrne's *The Secret*, in that I was trying to attract musicians to have sex with me by writing about having sex with them. Sometimes it was a true story.

To explain why I would do something so ill-advised, I should tell you I grew up in Slough. This is a deeply disappointing town in England. You might have been taught at school the John Betjeman poem that suggests friendly bombs should fall on it.

John was spot on. Whenever *I* think of Slough I think of that Divinyls song, 'Boys in Town', in which Chrissy Amphlett wishes she could get out of here. I figured that writing about my ideal life was my passport out. Certainly, it led to record companies granting me interviews with bands, which, like music festival bookers are always saying, I chose entirely based on merit. On the merit of their promo photos.

Slapper was a wink-nudge take on demented fandom. Issue one had no discernible theme, but interviews with super-groupies such as Pamela

Des Barres and Cynthia Plaster Caster. Issue two was the 'Cannibalistic Groupie' issue. Issue three was the 'Obsessive Fan' issue. With the wisdom of hindsight, it was born out of a rage that I couldn't be one of the boys, I could only sleep with them. And thus, this curious aggression when writing about them.

Interviewing bands was nerve-racking. I'd down a quarter-bottle of vodka for Dutch courage and get on the phone to pester record companies for interviews. The interview itself would be fuelled by foul blends of Dad's Southern Comfort diluted with Cinzano that I'd swig out of a shampoo bottle on the train to London. The day after an interview, I'd steel myself before pressing *play* on my massive tape-recorder, fast-forwarding through all the slurry: 'Do you get groupies, then?' to get to the meatier: 'What are your views on religion?' and the cunning genius of: 'You must get really sick of people asking you about drugs ...'

It was an okay read all the same. I'd been told by some lecherous music hack that *Slapper* was 'subversive'. And, once I'd looked that up, I'd gone to great lengths to live up to it. There were accounts of run-ins with riot grrrls and publicists, and tips on how to stalk rock stars. I'd tot up how much the record company spent on me in drinks and food, and run the tally throughout the interviews, also advising other writers on which record shops offered the best prices for those unwanted CDs.

No one got the joke back in Slough, though. Mum seemed to be getting angrier and angrier, if anything. She'd taken to frisking me every time I left the house, so that I'd have to hurl bottles onto the hedge below my bedroom window and then go downstairs to assume the frisk position before picking up the bounty outside. She was constantly having to use the PA at our local venue to see if I was in attendance – embarrassing for both of us, quite frankly – or scrape me off the pavement after a night of underage revelry.

While this was all fun and japes, I was deadly serious about writing and was an obsessive collector of underground press and counter-culture books. I admired the usual gonzo writers like Hunter S. Thompson and Anthony Burgess (whose *Clockwork Orange* style I'd nicked for *Slapper*), and your classic sexists like Bukowski and Roth. And then there were the heroes of the *New Musical Express*.

Steven Wells was an *NME* anarcho-journo who'd branched out into the national papers, and was fond of amphetamine-fuelled alliteration. He was famed for crucifying sweet young bands, mercilessly interrogating twee indie-popsters on their lack of political knowledge, and seamlessly segueing his hatred of Margaret Thatcher into most of his reviews. So I wrote to him. The letter was cute, funny and fawning – I thought – designed to emphasise our age gap and my relative naivety. Again, with hindsight, I was following that terrible tradition of the young female writer looking for a male ambassador.

Six months after writing to Steven (correspondence moved slowly pre-Twitter), the letter came. He was crafting a piece on young female fanzine writers for a weighty national periodical, the *Sunday Observer*. Where did I live? It didn't matter – he was prepared to come. I read it and read it again. I was insanely flattered he thought my work was up to the job and galloped downstairs to tell my mother, even as I mentally planned the author photo on the back of my first memoir.

When the big day came, I pulled my grooviest books to the front of my bookcases and hid the Enid Blyton. There was a fair bit of frantic vinyl arranging and some artful flinging around of clothes. A joss-stick might have been lit. Framed by our front door, Steven was gonzo personified – a rudely shaved head, glinting eyes, chest hair poking through his shirt, bad tattoos and a chemical energy. Mum came up to offer him a cup of tea and some biscuits. I pulled forth a wooden chair in my bedroom.

'So, you're quite posh, aren't you?' he said in bracing northern tones.

There was a silence while my brow furrowed. 'No.'

'Yes, you are – I've seen your mother.' He scraped his chair nearer and glowered. 'You're a child of Thatcher!'

He delivered a confusing rant about the poll tax, Tories and class war, punctuated with, 'You're a product of the '80s!' I'm not sure how he'd deduced my middle-classness from my letter – maybe I'd used Mum's Basildon Bond writing paper – but he clearly had his agenda all set out. Even so, I was desperate to deliver, so I mentioned the one unsatisfactory fumble with a musician I'd genuinely had, which had been more by accident than by design. He wasn't happy with just this. 'But what sort of bloke do you fancy?' he asked impatiently.

I looked him up and down before answering. 'Huge, hulking, hairy-chested, scowling, tattooed monsters,' I said. Somewhere, a death knell tolled.

———

If it had been the *Slough Observer*, it'd probably have been all right. As it was, Steven's piece took up most of page three of the national *Sunday Observer*. 'More sex please, we're groupies – and proud of it!' screamed the headline. The crux of the piece – in well-formed quotes that simply couldn't have come out of my mouth – was that I thought groupies were a maligned sort, and people who thought groupies were degrading themselves were just ignorant. There was a pull-quote under my picture: 'I'm not after plastic hunks. I'm after real rock'n'roll men. Huge, hulking, hairy-chested, scowling, tattooed monsters. Phwoarr!'

As if I'd have said, 'Phwoarr.'

Steven had done what all journalists aspire to do – coined a new movement. I was now spearheading the new breed of middle-class groupie – a SWAT team of crack stage-door botherers. And Britain's first 'sexzine', *Slapper*, was their bible. I noticed his other case studies, Philippa (who greeted *Slapper* as 'a real breath of fresh air') and Jill ('working-class boys know how to handle women!'), hadn't been stupid enough to have *their* pictures taken.

Oh, because the picture was equally damning. I'd recently shorn my hair and my fringe had coincidentally peaked into devil horns, while at my feet was a splayed arrangement of *Slapper*s. I'd quite clearly posed for this.

'Why's Mum crying in the rose bushes?' my brother asked on his visit home from uni. He stood perplexed at the door of my bedroom as I continued to scour the mash-up, my initial hilarity gradually being overtaken by something more anxious. The bad feeling intensified as I read the pull-quote one more time.

Poor Mum. Over the last few years her features had been drawn into an arrangement of furious anticipation, like a Greek tragedy mask. And there was more heartache to come, my brother informed me, when he'd stopped laughing long enough. Our grandparents read the paper. Then there was Mum's art class, her classics class, her book group ... okay, we were quite middle-class, come to think of it.

Dad paid my bedroom a rare visit and cleared his throat. 'You've really shafted your mother this time,' he said in his most businesslike voice. We left it at that.

Two hours later, Mum opened the boot of her car like a Louis Vuitton handbag hawker and turfed out eighty copies of the *Sunday Observer*, hauled in over a four-mile radius.

When driving me anywhere over the next few weeks, Mum throttled the handbrake like she was wringing the neck of a chicken and didn't observe speed limits. At home she banged cupboard doors, one by one. Steven's revelation that I'd been writing the fanzine for years launched a new paranoia that she'd lose her job at Social Services due to my teenage sexiness.

Luckily I was about to move out. Unluckily, everyone at uni had already seen the article, right down to my new flatmates.

Over the next few months I received endless requests for interviews from newspapers and TV shows. When I declined to answer I was used in braying beat-ups all the same, and one magazine invited debate on my sluttiness. Sometimes a journalist would lift text from Steven's masterpiece, or they'd get more imaginative. A highbrow paper pitted me against the singer of Iron Maiden, Bruce Dickinson, by asking the hoary rocker what he thought of girls who said things like: 'I'm not after plastic hunks. I'm after real rock'n'roll men. Huge, hulking, hairy-chested, scowling, tattooed monsters. Phwoarr!' Bruce was scathing.

The Sunday Times jumped enthusiastically onto Steven's new breed of middle-class groupie idea and swiped it for the cover of their 'Style' supplement. 'Spot the groupie: vice girl or nice girl?' it said, over a photograph of a demure young lady in a tunic.

In an attempt at damage control, a music PR company, for which I'd become something of a mascot, cherry-picked some more sympathetic music mags for me so I could tell my non-story again. But as Princess Di might have told you back then, you can't control the press. Interviews seemed to go well enough. The phrase 'A labour of love, then?' would get tossed up in an admiring tone, and the finished copy would say something like: 'In person, Jenny doesn't look like butter, let alone a guitarist's tricep, would melt in her mouth.'

By now I was getting self-pitying. While I wasn't leading a dignified life, I was way too drunk to be doing all the things people implied, and any PR chick worth her salt would be getting more sexy band action than I was. The media was obsessed with new genres of women, and I'd fallen foul of this race to slap on a fresh label, whether it be riot grrrls, Sloane Rangers or ladettes.

'Why don't you capitalise on it?' one journalist demanded once in a West London cafe after I'd told her my sorry predicament. 'Run with it!' she urged in exasperation. '*Become* Jenny Slapper.'

But *Slapper* was fast becoming ridiculously out of step with my belief system. By this time I was sending off for copies of Valerie Solanas' *Scum Manifesto* and Andrea Dworkin texts. And so I dyed my hair a no-room-for-misunderstandings black and aborted *Slapper*. It was a sad time.

These days I'm a newspaper journalist myself, and while I've occasionally incurred the irritation of an interviewee, my own moment of infamy has shaped my desire to handle people's stories with great care. You could say it's even become a mission – I'm a member of AOD (Alcohol and Other Drugs) Media Watch, which has a team of researchers and clinicians that responds to stigmatising, inaccurate and salacious stories about drug use.

Incidentally, I wrote about this story a while back and I gave Steven Wells the right of reply. A sense of propriety prevents me from then having the last word, so I will bid you adieu here.

'What a superbly deranged (if over-long) rant,' he answered. 'Having created an amusing alter ego – following in the footsteps of Poly Styrene and Johnny Rotten – you cried foul the first time anyone outside a tight little circle of fanzine buyers took Jenny Slapper at face value. I thought you were punk, turned out you were indie. Basically, you bottled it. Shame on you, Jenny.'

Catastrophically Stupid

Susan Carland

I HAVE MANY CATASTROPHES I can draw on. My life seems to contain an inordinate number of embarrassing events. I just seem to specialise in humiliating myself. It's a gift. For this reason, it's hard to know which story to share with you.

But the one I've decided to share is particularly humiliating because it was a time when I was trying to act my cleverest. It was a time when I desperately wanted to prove how smart I was, but ended up looking my most moronic. And the universe seems to have that very Australian sense of humour in demolishing anyone who's getting a bit too big for their boots, doesn't it?

I give you: exhibit A.

So, come with me now. Let us all climb aboard the SS *Mortification Memory* for a jolly boatride into the sea of my embarrassment. It was many years ago. I was in my twenties and looking for validation in all the wrong places. Namely, the ABC.

I got a call from a producer at a now defunct show called *The Einstein Factor*. Possibly the nerdiest show on the nerdiest channel, it was a quiz show that tested contestants on both general knowledge and their field of expertise. Pitted against the contestants was the Brains Trust, a collection of 'personalities'. The producer wanted me as a guest on the Brains Trust. It was my big moment! My chance to show myself as Officially Smart, as endorsed by the national public broadcaster.

I picked out a darling hijab to wear – stylish, yet serious. It gave a touch of excitement but still conveyed the message, 'I conceal a massive brain.' I was going to be on with Jennifer Byrne! We'd probably become best friends.

I was desperately hoping I would do a stellar job and be brought on as a regular panellist for the Brains Trust. I imagined myself as a contracted employee of the ABC, laughing and getting coffee with the other members of the Brains Trust. We'd be a whatever the collective noun was for a group of geniuses. A factorial? An elite?

My first task was to tell my father. I wanted to impress him. His TV was permanently tuned to the ABC, so I figured he'd be thrilled.

'Dad, guess what? *Einstein Factor* want me to be on their Brains Trust!'
Silence.

'You? Really?' my stunned dad finally said. 'Are you sure they didn't want Waleed? That's what I would have assumed.'

Cheers, Dad.

Determined to prove myself to my father in a way that would make a psychoanalyst giggle, I invited him to come to the taping. This would prove to him unequivocally just how clever I was. I picked up my skeptical father and we drove off to Ripponlea, the old home of the ABC in Melbourne. I was nervous. I felt I had a lot to prove. There was a lot riding on this.

We finally arrived at the studio and had to negotiate a complicated series of boom gates to enter the carpark. The building was old, the carpark narrow, packed and winding. I finally found a spot and started to ease my way in. My dad started to protest but I was determined to at least park before I listened to any more of his complaints, thank you very much.

For God's sake, Dad, I can at least park a car without you telling me I can't do that either!

Crunch.

I'd backed into a car behind me that I hadn't noticed.

At the very moment when I was trying to prove to my father that I was smart and capable, I had hit a parked car. In one awkward manoeuvre in my manual blue Hyundai hatch, I had shown myself to my dad as being everything I was trying not to be: clumsy, foolish, incapable.

I may have, through clenched teeth, muttered some words most unbefitting of a practising Muslim woman.

'I was trying to tell you —' my father started.

Yes, cheers, Dad.

Now I had to go in and alert whoever owned the car I had smashed. Leaving my dad alone so he could really focus on my ineptitude uninterrupted, I ran into the ABC building to find the car's owner.

'Please let it be someone irrelevant to the show. Please let it be some guy from HR, or a woman from accounts. Let it be the security guard. Please just don't let it be someone connected to a show called *The Einstein Factor* whom I am trying to suitably impress with my intellect so they make me a regular on the Brains Trust,' I was saying to myself.

The owner of the car was located. It was none other than the executive producer of the show. I introduced myself and explained that I had managed to smash her safely parked car.

'Which is funny, isn't it?' I said meekly. 'Given I'm here to be a smart person on a smart show, ha, ha, ha ...' I trailed off.

It was the most humiliated I had ever felt. It was one of those moments that you fervently hope is just a bad dream. But this was none other than a colossal moment of shame.

As the newest member of the Brains Trust I distinguished myself as a comprehensive idiot who could not even manage to enter the building without causing major destruction and my own humiliation. I don't really remember much about how the show went after that. I do know that I received the bill for the car repairs from the EP and did not receive an invitation back to the Brains Trust.

Two Eyeballs.
One Job. No Brain

Marc Fennell

MARC FENNELL IS my name, but for many years I had another name. It was heard by millions; it was yelled at me from passing cars. If I was at a music festival or a bar, at some point someone would be sure to come up to me and say, 'Hey, are you that movie guy?'

There was the time I was standing in a toilet queue, facing a quizzical look from a woman who stood there for a good forty-five seconds before she went, 'Oh, that movie guy.'

I said, 'Yes.'

'Omigod, I'm so relieved,' she audibly exhaled. 'I thought I'd slept with you.'

For fourteen years I was a film critic at FBI and then Triple J, known as 'That movie guy'. Perhaps it is the only thing I'll ever be known for. I lucked into being a film reviewer when I was seventeen, and it was a hobby that just stuck and became a career.

I feel it's important to point out that I have no actual qualifications. My greatest achievements are taking two and a half months of a Media Communications Degree and the fact that I have watched every single episode of *Star Trek: Voyager*. If you don't think that's an achievement, then you have not struggled through season two.

I'm going to tell you something: you don't need a lot of skill to be Australia's leading film critic for eighteen to twenty-four year-olds. I could describe a plot in under fifteen seconds, I was highly proficient in low-key snark and I could dole out them three and half star ratings like it was nobody's business. But there is one thing you do need in this job. You need eyes. This is the story of the time I comprehensively fucked one of the very few prerequisites for my career.

The year was 2009, I think. I woke up and my long-suffering girlfriend, now extremely long-suffering wife, had gone to work, because she had a proper job. I opened my eyes and almost the moment I could feel the sun peering through the window I knew something was wrong. Any light passing into my eyes sent a searing pain right through my head. I had never felt anything like it before. I went through the house, closing all of the blinds and sat in darkness. What the fuck had I done?

I started timing how long I could open my eyes before they would spasm shut. I tried to have a closer look at them in a mirror, but I'm incredibly short-sighted. Without being able to put my contact lenses in I would have to climb onto the sink and go right up to the bathroom mirror – actually, I'd have to hold onto the bathroom mirror – to find the depth of field to make out what was happening with my eyes. And so I did exactly that. Straddled on either side of the basin, I hugged the mirror, and as I opened my eyes I feared the worse. Would my corneas be that opaque white you see in movies when people go blind? Three, two, one … open.

What I saw shocked me. There was no white left. There was no pink. There was blood red surrounding my corneas. That was when I decided to call Terry.

Let me tell you about Terry. I like to say Elton John introduced me to Terry, because when I was in year 3 my dad took me to my very first concert – Elton John. (Because I am incredibly cool.) There in the nosebleeds, Dad asked me halfway through 'Benny and the Jets', 'Hey, whaddya think?'

I said, 'Sounds good.'

'But like whaddya think about the concert?' He gestured to what I assume was a vast and elaborate stage extravaganza, which to me, 'undiagnosed short-sighted child', was a gigantic multicoloured blur.

Again I said, 'Sounds good!'

And so Dad took me to my new optometrist, Terry. Terry was this no-bullshit kind of guy in Burwood, who gave me my first glasses and contact lenses.

If ever there was a time for Terry, this was it. Over the phone, I explained the situation to Terry, who in his broad, thick accent said, 'That doesn't sound good. Come on in. Oh, and bring your contacts with you.'

Great. I have a plan. There'll be an ointment or something for this ... Oh fuck. How am I going to get to Terry?

I toyed with the idea of driving, and when I say toyed, I mean I went down to the garage, got in the car, turned the key, opened the garage door. It burns, the sun ... it burns ... I had become Dracula.

A new plan – public transport. Through a complex process of only opening my eyes in fifteen to twenty second intervals, I managed to cross a major road, accidentally walk into three front yards, and not fall onto the tracks of Lewisham train station. By now I was starting to enter that phase where I thought, okay, I can't see but maybe my other senses have become heightened. Maybe I can hear a crime three suburbs away.

I finally made it to Terry's. In his specially darkened room, he sat me in his examination chair, peeled my eyelids apart and shone a light in ... and took a deep, confused breath.

Terry was a fine, upstanding member of the Chinese community in Burwood and a consummate professional, so he would never say the words that I just knew he was thinking ... 'What the fuck have you done?' He then asked to see my contacts.

The moment he began unscrewing the lid I knew what I'd done. I realised how badly I'd fucked this up. He pulled out the little round plastic lens and held it to the light. There was a beat ... He knew it too. One of us had to speak.

'Marc,' Terry said, 'how long have you been wearing these for?'

'Oh ... um ... six months.'

'Marc, you know they're monthlies, right?'

'Oh, really?'

The worst part was that six months was a lie. I had been wearing them for at least eighteen months. In that time, we would discover, calcifications had built up on the plastic. Scans would later reveal that they had dug tiny craters in my cornea. Under a microscope, my eyeballs looked like the surface of the moon – bashed and battered with the asteroids of my own searing incompetence.

I wish there was a word for the experience of sitting in front of a medical professional when you have been diagnosed but there is not yet a prognosis. Surely there is a word in German for that moment, when your mind jumps to the worst-case scenario. I thought, I'm fucked. I can do one thing and I need my eyes to do it, and I've ruined it forever because I was too lazy to go and get new contacts.

I was silently hyperventilating and Terry looked at me with an expression that seemed to say, 'I've checked the back cupboard and I am fresh outta fucks to give.' In fact, by that point, I'm quite sure the number of fucks Terry was giving had entered deep negative integers.

But he was incredibly professional and prescribed some medicated eye drops and handed me a pair of glasses. Then, in the same manner that a parent chastises a disobedient child or a dog that's just shat in the living room, Terry said, 'I am never prescribing you contact lenses again.'

That week of being semi-blind had a number of unexpected consequences. First, I got addicted to Twitter. Only open your eyes for thirty seconds, say something bitchy, ouch it burns. I also sat in my dark apartment filled with movies and came up with my first book.

After a year of wearing glasses, a TV producer came up to me and said, 'Hey, you should really wear contacts. Glasses just add an extra layer of wanker that you just don't need.' So I decided it was time to go back to Terry for the last time.

I begged him for contacts. We struck a deal – dailies. Daily contact lenses that I wear to this day. A few months after this, Terry was on a golf course and had a heart attack and died.

I still get my contacts from Terry's shop; his son works there now. And to this day, every time I go to bed and flick out those contacts, as I close my eyes I see Terry's incredulous look of disapproval, and I cannot help but smile.

The Kangaroo Is Still Alive

Kirstie Clements

IT SHOULD BE smooth sailing when you're the editor of a glossy fashion magazine, sitting at your gold desk, sipping champagne and matching belts to outfits. Enter the fashion editors, men and women who live in another world. It is made up of a sea of Emma Bovarys who are not satisfied with reality. As one fashion director said to me seriously one day when I was questioning a shoot budget, 'I always think if you're going to spend $5000, you may as well spend $10,000.' Stylists don't live in the real world. They don't like the real world. They want the real world to be better – don't we all?

As the editor, you're in charge of the money. And the stylists, they're in charge of wasting it. In fact, most of my job wasn't doing all the fabulous stuff you'd assume it would involve. Most of my time as editor at *Vogue Australia* was spent upstairs battling management. I'm not using names in order to protect the identities of the deluded.

Let me tell you about one particular shoot in South Africa.

I got an email one day. 'We'd like to offer you a trip to South Africa.' Shooting, shooting, editorial, lovely, lovely, lovely. I took it to my then fashion director.

'That'll be great,' she said, 'but I don't want to go to South Africa. I want to go to Botswana.'

'But the trip that's been offered is to South Africa.'

'Botswana has better animals.'

'Okay, right, so South Africa is free, Botswana isn't.'

This particular stylist always attracted trouble. We used to call her 'If it wasn't one thing it was always another'. She decided one day that it was crucial to have a certain Polish supermodel feature in *Vogue Australia*. The model was already coming to Australia and we had to get her for the magazine. And she was coming in with her boyfriend.

'Oh, okay, great,' I said.

'Oh, no, actually we have to pay for their fares now' … 'Oh, no, now it's business class.'

So we paid for business-class airfares for both of them, even though they were coming anyway. Well, that was awesome. And we had to put them up in a hotel – The Intercontinental, mind you.

In the middle of the night they changed hotels because they didn't like the decor and went to The Four Seasons. We paid.

The stylist decided they had to go to a desert location, and that required a light plane. They love excess baggage on light planes. So now they were going to the middle of Australia, the Polish supermodel and her boyfriend. And my poor deputy editor. She was the one who had to endure the torture, not me. Back in the office, when it was finally over, all she wanted to do was go home and take a Valium.

They needed to go out on a recky and they'd been told not to drive after dark for various reasons, one of which was that you could hit a kangaroo. So they went driving after dark in a convoy of two, maybe three, jeeps (I'm sure when I signed off the bills there were three) and they hit a kangaroo. The supermodel completely freaked out. She's vegan. She's an animal lover. She hasn't eaten for months. So, she asked, 'Is the kangaroo all right?' The crew knew the kangaroo was not all right.

'Yes,' they told her, 'the kangaroo's going to be fine.'

She went back to the hotel and said, 'I can't shoot if there's something wrong with that kangaroo. I won't be shooting.'

The crew rallied in the bar, wondering what to do. It was late at night when they went back to find the kangaroo. It was dead, unfortunately, so they dragged it off the road and buried it, because they had to drive that same route the next day.

In the hotel bar the supermodel was absolutely traumatised, until they said, 'We went back and we did some stuff and we just rubbed it and it hopped away.'

'Oh, okay. I guess I can shoot in the morning, then.'

When they woke up the next morning it had rained, and it hadn't rained in Lake Eyre for three years. So they couldn't shoot. And that was that.

Animals often got in the way of our shoots. You know the old saying, 'Never work with animals or children.' We didn't work with children often, but we did work with animals a lot. Once the fashion crew and the stylists were out of your sight, it was a free-for-all. I'd sign off all the trips and then wonder: What are the team doing in Egypt today? Oh, they're doing a camel casting. They are literally casting for camels? I thought they'd just get one that wasn't as mangey as the others, but the casting took half a day.

My favourite time was when editors were about to go away and we'd do what's called a 'run-through'. We'd go into the fashion stock room where all the clothes were hanging and all the accessories were lined up. It was a bit like Meryl Streep in *The Devil Wears Prada*. I'd ask, 'What are you shooting? Where are you shooting? Who are you shooting?' And remind them that it was all about product, product, product. It's a business, after all.

I sent two young fashion editors to Bali for seven days to shoot two stories. We'd done the big run-through and it was all about merchandise, merchandise, merchandise.

Being a nice boss, I said, 'You know what, girls? This will be an intense couple of shoots, so you can stay an extra day and just relax and come back that night.'

So they came back and they were really tanned.

'Can I see the pictures?' I said.

'Yeah, sure.'

I look at the shots, and say, 'Where are the clothes?'

'Yeah, so we changed the brief. We decided to do nudes.'

'Woah, twenty-seven pages of nudes. I can see a bikini bottom there, what advertiser is that?'

'Oh, no. That's vintage.'

My last 'stylists gone wild' story is my favourite. It was Greece 2000, just before the Olympics; a big Greece story with lots of supermodels. We flew over with a stylist I wasn't entirely sure of, and I was there to keep an eye on the whole thing. I had briefed everyone – *I want glamour, I want this, I want that. I want shiny. I want blue hair. I want navy and white stripes. I want red lipstick and gold sandals. I want the whole Mykonos vibe.*

There we were in Mykonos, in a beautiful 5-star hotel, and everything seemed perfect.

But the stylist hated me.

They said to me, 'We're just going in the van to find a spot for the shoot, then we're going to send the van back to get you.'

Fine. So I was sitting in this beautiful hotel, reading *The Colossus of Maroussi* by Henry Miller, you know, trying to get in the Greece zone. Time passed. No van.

The van never came back. I didn't know where they were, but I tried not to panic. I knew that I had briefed and briefed and briefed up the wazoo about what I wanted to see, so it should be fine.

Eventually they returned and I said, 'So you got some glamorous pictures?'

'Yeah, they're awesome. They are great. You're going to love them.'

It was digital, post-polaroid, so I couldn't really see anything ... until we were back in Sydney. They had driven the model to what appeared to be an abandoned, bombed field. It looked like it had been in a nuclear explosion. There was a gypsy caravan and beside it, a burning oil drum, and they took the shots next to it. God knows what I spent on that trip. I had to go up to management and say, 'Look at these amazing pictures,' with a straight face.

Vogue attracts really great talent and it attracts completely fucking crazy people. There are some stylists you don't even know are working for you.

I got a phone call one day from Harley Davidson, and it went like this.

'Hi, this is Harley Davidson.'

'Hi.'

'When are we getting our bikes back?'

'Umm, I don't know … where are your bikes?'

'Well, your fashion editor came in this week and borrowed two Harleys.'

'All right, did you get some paperwork, a business card or anything?'

'No, no we didn't.'

'How did that happen?'

'He came and put two bikes on the back of a van and then he drove off, and I was expecting them back.'

'I'm sorry, we haven't borrowed any Harleys for a shoot. Can you tell me what this person looked like?'

'Well, he stood out from my usual customers.'

'Why was that?'

'Well, he was dressed in women's clothes.'

'He was dressed in women's clothes?'

'Yes, and he had high heels on.'

'Oh, okay.'

'And he had this thing, this feather thing around his neck.'

'A feather boa?'

'Yes.'

They had literally given two Harley Davidson motorbikes to this marvellous guy, who clearly fitted their mental image of a *Vogue* stylist.

Then it happened again. A jeweller rang me.

'Kirstie, when are the jewels and the diamonds and the Rolexs coming back from the shoot?'

'I don't know what you're talking about.'

'Your stylist borrowed them this morning and we're expecting them back, because you only borrowed them for the day. And now it's four o'clock.'

'I don't know what you're talking about, there is no shoot,' I said.

And she said, 'No, no, no, Michael borrowed them.'

'Who's Michael?'

'The *Vogue* stylist Michael,' she said.

'We don't have a Michael. You know better than this, to give away jewels.'

'But,' she said, 'he's been coming in for eighteen months.'

Over an eighteen-month period this man Michael would go to the shop to borrow things, take them away and then return them. On this particular sting, he had five different jewellers lined up whom he'd been visiting all that time, and they trusted him because he'd been handing the stuff back.

Unfortunately, he'd recruited a young woman. He'd put an ad in the paper saying, 'I'm a *Vogue* stylist and I need an assistant' and this woman had answered it. She was only nineteen. He made her collect all the jewels, so that it was her face on the camera. Then he told her to meet him at an intersection in Paddington between one and two o'clock, carrying millions of dollars' worth of jewellery. When he collected them from her, he got into a taxi and it drove off, leaving her wondering, Where's the shoot?

She was smart enough to call *Vogue*. When she came in, she started to hyperventilate and had a complete panic attack; we had to call an ambulance. She was on my floor, on oxygen, and I had jewellers calling me, asking, 'Where are the Rolexs?' 'Where is the Cartier?'

The man was eventually arrested, and it turns out he only had one arm. So he was literally a one-armed bandit.

Finally, the scam that I like to call 'Puccigate'.

A young junior assistant, who was smart and devious enough to make her way into our office from another department, put in a request for a couture bridal gown from Pucci. Now, your relationships with the overseas suppliers are tenuous. You have to be so careful and make sure that everything is sent back within twenty-four hours, wrapped in tissue. Anyway, this young woman said she was with *Vogue* and on her request, Pucci sent her a $35,000 couture dress.

A short time passed and Pucci called us, asking where their dress was, and all we could say was, 'We don't know what you're talking about.'

My deputy started to investigate and someone said to her, 'I think this girl over in another department has requested it.'

We got on her Facebook page and found out she was getting married soon. So we went over to her department.

'Do you maybe have a Pucci dress?'

'No, I don't.'

'Oh, you don't, but that's your signature on the form.'

'No, no, no.'

We had to get to the bottom of this, so my deputy kept riding her. Pucci were on our case every day and we were trying to pretend nothing had happened. 'Oh, the couture dress – where could it be? I think it's on a shoot.'

Meanwhile, the young woman kept saying, 'No, no, no.'

As it turns out, she had stuffed it in a drawer at home. Knowing we were on to her, she pulled it out and put it in a post bag. This was a $35,000 dress that needed to be archived. When we found out what was going on, we said to Pucci, 'It's going back to you, but perhaps not in the way you're expecting, and maybe, just maybe, you're not going to be that thrilled.'

Then it got lost. Of course it did. It was lost in London.

I had to go up to management and tell them what had happened. Management had zero idea of what we did downstairs every day, and they said, 'Who cares?'

'I do,' I said. 'If it were me I would fire her, but that would just be me.'

As it transpires, at the end of it all, she went off on sick leave and sued us for stress.

Do I Smell?

Kate McClymont

A S I CHATTED to people in the foyer, I kept a close watch on them. Were they breathing through their mouths? Did they involuntarily take a step back when I came near?

In short, do I smell?

The reason for my anxiety is that – although I only ever write the nicest things about the loveliest of people – of late some of these people have been making rather unpleasant remarks suggesting a catastrophic failure in my personal hygiene.

A couple Saturdays ago, there I was fast asleep when my phone beeped. Who could be sending me a text at 1.46 am?

It was Eddie Hayson and he was texting to tell me I was a 'dirty unwashed beast'.

It is tragic enough to be called a beast, but to be called a dirty unwashed beast by that pillar of the sporting world, Eddie Hayson, is, in my mind, catastrophic. After all, just because Eddie Hayson is a former bankrupt, brothel-owning chronic gambler who has been banned from every TAB in the country and from Sydney's Star Casino, and who may or may not be involved in match fixing, does not mean he hasn't got an acute sense of smell.

Was he lying awake, tossing and turning in the wee hours of the morning thinking someone really has to tell her? Especially given that the previous week he was trying to do me a favour. On a quiet Sunday afternoon Eddie Hayson accidentally sent me a message saying: 'Race 5 Port Macquarie no 2 Urban Prince. Get on it.'

I jokingly replied: 'We are set at ten large.'

Realising his message had not been delivered to its intended recipient, Hayson responded: 'If you had any brains you would be.'

Meanwhile, I looked up the race field in Port Macquarie and suggested Eddie would be better to put his money on a horse called Before You Think.

As for Urban Prince, well it wasn't such a sure thing after all, coming in at third place. When I pointed out his tip was a dud he replied, 'You got the jockey to pull it up, didn't you?'

I think back about other people and their hurtful remarks. Were they also trying to tell me something? Were they merely being cruel to be kind? Take Jamie Vincent, the son of underworld figure Teflon Tony Vincent.

We were outside the Downing Centre Court and Jamie arrived – 100 kilograms of muscle, a bullet head, leather jacket and the obligatory dark glasses. I mentioned to our photographer that the Vincents were not particularly nice and they had murdered people in the past. And since Jamie was about to be sent to jail for the third time he might not be in the best of moods, so if he was going to take a photo of Jamie Vincent, better to err on the side of caution and not get too close. With that I blithely set off to get a coffee. I returned to find the photographer ashen-faced and shaking.

'What's the matter?' I asked.

Jamie Vincent had come over to the photographer and, leaning within inches of his face, had said, 'If you publish any photos of me, I will come after you. I will track you down and I will get you.'

'Listen, mate, I am just doing my job. Don't shoot the messenger,' said the photographer, rather foolishly.

'But I will shoot the messenger,' said Vincent.

At this point I marched over to old bullet-head, who was standing in the queue waiting to go through the court's security check.

'How dare you threaten my photographer!' I snapped.

'Listen, you stinking ugly old hag, why don't you piss off!' Vincent snarled.

There it was again. I wasn't just an ugly old hag, I was a smelly one.

And recently a charming man, Andrew Saab, described me on Facebook as – among other things – an 'effing red neck whore' and a 'bush pig'. I wondered if bush pigs smell more than normal ones.

Andrew Saab is the brother of Majid Saab. And Majid Saab, who threatened me outside the lifts at ICAC, is the charming son-in-law of my other favourite Eddie, Edward Moses Obeid, former MP and now convicted criminal.

Summer is approaching and most Australians like to go away for Christmas. But Eddie Obeid has been doing everything he can to stop going away over Christmas. Maybe that is because 'going away' for him would be a stint in jail after being found guilty of corrupt conduct earlier in the year.

Over the last few years Eddie Obeid and his family have been the subject of no less that five corruption hearings before the Independent Commission Against Corruption. And I have been there for every one.

It was on one such day – Thursday, 21 August 2014, to be precise – that I suffered the full catastrophe. I had just received word from our publishers that due to the wrong Chris Brown being identified in our recently published book *He Who Must Be Obeid*, the book would have to be pulped. It was just plain wrong and there was no one to blame but myself.

So there was I, sitting in ICAC feeling devastated and shell-shocked about the book, when a text message flashed onto my screen.

'Hi Kate, It's John Ibrahim her [sic] could u pls send me a copy of ur book that be nice … thank u.'

'Very funny! Who is this really?' I replied.

It really was the Kings Cross identity, who was keen to get a copy of the book before it was too late.

As I was thinking of replying to John Ibrahim that he would now be able to buy the book on the black market like everyone else, another text came through. It was the police. They needed to talk to me about the Obeids. Finally, some good news in an otherwise shocking day, I thought.

Wrong!

The police had just come from the Obeids' house.

'You have no idea how much they hate you,' an officer told me.

'I think I do,' I said.

The police officer said, 'No, I don't think you do.'

According to the police, one of the many things the Obeids were accusing me of was sending them death threats. Death threats! I could scarcely believe my ears. I had just written a tell-all book on the Obeids, even though it was about to be pulped. Why would I be sending them death threats?

I had received an email from a person calling himself Peter Ryan. It read: 'Tip: Fast Eddie has a McGurk contract heading his way. Keep your eyes and ears open.'

This was a reference to the 2009 contract killing of businessman Michael McGurk. The week before he was killed, McGurk had told me that there was a contract out on his life but – to my endless regret – I had thought he was merely attention seeking.

I wasn't about to make the same mistake again. So I queried the mysterious Mr Ryan, who replied that the contract on Obeid 'has been offered around for a while and his card is marked'.

I went to the police with the emails, and their visit to the ICAC hearing was to fill me in on their investigation about the death threats. They said the emails had been sent from an internet cafe in Bondi. But there the trail had gone dead. Whoever had sent the emails had opened an account in a fake name, using a mobile phone that had also been set up using a false name.

It did not matter what the police said, the Obeids were convinced that I was responsible for the death threats. Somehow I was racing out of the ICAC hearings, heading to a Bondi internet cafe, sending an email to myself, and then racing back to Bondi to reply. And, of course, passing these on to the police.

The very suggestion of this sent my children into a fit of derisive laughter. On one occasion I had arrived at ICAC in a complete state because my phone was missing. I looked everywhere, I retraced my steps, I employed 'find my phone', to no avail. Later that day I received a call from home. My family had some good news and some bad news. The good news was they had found my phone. The bad news was it was in the oven and it was cooked. It was now a baked Apple. Don't even ask!

The very idea that I could use my technological genius to send death threats about the Obeids to myself was beyond ludicrous. But as my family said, there is always good news and bad news. For every catastrophe there is a coup. Not only is the book *He Who Must Be Obeid* back on the shelf but the first-edition copies are on eBay for triple the initial price.

And as for the real He Who Must Be Obeid, hopefully by year's end he'll be trying out his skills of persuasion courtesy of Her Majesty's pleasure.

Editor's note:
Eddie is indeed on the inside, where the sun still shines and perhaps the perfumed roses grow.

Woman, Interrupted

Emma Alberici

Editor's note:

Emma told this story in the middle of the ABC scandal involving ABC managing director Michelle Guthrie and chair of the ABC Board Justin Milne. After writing a piece about how some of Australia's largest corporations avoid paying tax, her journalism was under attack from the prime minister, the Coalition government and the chair of the ABC, who allegedly told his MD to 'get rid of her'. In the midst of the fiasco, one commentator criticised Emma for being a 'woman of considerable self-belief'. We were considering getting t-shirts printed emblazoned with this message. So here's Emma, battered and bruised but never bowed, embracing a different catastrophe.

LET ME TELL you everything I know about corporate tax.

Don't be silly, everyone knows I don't know anything about corporate tax.

So, rather than pretend I can distinguish between profit and revenue, I'm going to stick to the topic of being a mum and a wife, specifically the time when being a wife and a mum made me a national hero.

I'm exaggerating, but that happens when you have too much self-belief.

In 2008 I became the first Australian mother posted overseas as a foreign correspondent. It was a dream job and I had dreamt about it since I was at university, where I did a lowly Arts degree majoring in Italian. I had to go through a rigorous interview process with an earnest panel asking me about the origins of the global financial crisis and calling on comparisons with the 1930s Depression. As FDR said back then, the only thing I had to fear was fear itself. I was breastfeeding a four-month-old baby at the time but I had multi-tasking down pat. The prospect of being the ABC's Europe correspondent was the reason I joined the ABC back in 2002, after meeting the then new director Max Uechtritz on a flight back from Canberra, where I'd been the tally-room reporter for the federal election. He hired me to host a show called *Business Breakfast*. I went on to become the finance editor for *7.30*. By the time I was sitting in that boardroom talking about the Depression I had three children under three.

Big ups to the ABC News management; not only did they give me the job despite the fact I was on maternity leave, but I beat six other candidates who were all men, who may or may not have been fathers. That detail was as unremarkable then as it is now. Being a father isn't, hasn't and will most likely never be career limiting.

So, I got this ace gig and I was feeling pretty happy about my life, notwithstanding the fact that we had just demolished a house, started a renovation, and were about to lay new foundations. My then husband Jason was working as a sound recordist for, wait for it, *Australia's Next Top Model*. There was no way he was going to give that job up to organise logistics for London.

The ABC had me doing countless shifts of training in technology for use out in the field, and a hostile-environment course about what to do if you are bombed or kidnapped. And then there were those three small people to consider. Who had the time to choose schools and make living arrangements? I'm still astonished that an organisation as big as the ABC has no department for helping people move overseas.

After I'd come off my high from getting the job I shifted to thinking, 'Cripes, where do we live in London? Where do they go to school? What about childcare?'

I called the Head of International and his secretary said he'd call me back. I didn't hear from him for a day. So I emailed him.

Dear Mr International
Thanks again for this fantastic opportunity but you've only given me six weeks to get to the ABC bureau and start working. Where will we live? What arrangements shall I make for the kids? Is there someone in HR? Do I hire an agent when we get there?

Two days went by and no response. My initial euphoria began turning to anxiety, and I had a five-month-old by this stage so I was chronically sleep deprived, which was a toxic combination. Perhaps they didn't want me to take this job? Finally, one morning I marched up to Mr International's office and sat outside the glass doors, making his assistant a little uncomfortable. He arrived, made some excuse or other and then rather exasperatingly said, 'Emma, stop asking me all these questions. I don't have the answers. Normally the wives work it out.'

I was the first correspondent with children who didn't have a wife. For a moment I paused and imagined a world where you can have all that stuff handled, such as the childcare, being there for the plumber to arrive between seven and five, someone to collect the children from soccer, dancing, rugby, swimming or their mate's place. Imagine what it would be like to outsource all of that and not have to pay for it.

We packed up our lives and put all our belongings under four headings: *Sydney storage, London luggage, London air, London sea.*

Just getting to the airport that night in January 2008 was prize worthy. We had fourteen pieces of luggage and three small children, and it was already past their bedtime. We boarded the flight and put half our lives in the overhead lockers, and I could see the blood drain from the faces of the people around us.

After a stopover in Bangkok, we dressed the kids in Qantas pajamas and were told over the loudspeaker that we'd be served dinner after take-off and all was going to plan. But take-off didn't happen because the catering truck had smashed into the plane.

For an hour we sat on the tarmac. Then we were told that dinner would be served while they fixed the ding on the plane. We ate and were relieved when we heard from the captain that it would be just one more hour before we took off for London. We'd now been on the tarmac for three hours and the children were restless. I reached for the Phenergan. Baby Pia was too young to be drugged, but I gave Allegra and Miles a little more than a full dose each. And within fifteen minutes we had three sleeping children, much to the delight of our fellow passengers. By that time we should have been about to take off. Right? Wrong. Those aviation panel beaters had decided this quickie repair wasn't a good idea after all. We were informed that Qantas was shouting us all a day in Bangkok because it was 5 am. We'd be taking off for London at 10 pm. Oh my god.

We had to get off the plane with three sleeping children, our carry-on bags and collect fourteen pieces of luggage from the baggage carousel. We collared a woman who'd smiled at us on the plane, which was a rare pleasantry. We literally handed her the baby as we didn't have enough arms for everyone. At the Customs queue, after all the maelstrom of exiting the plane, she handed Pia back.

Oh, yeah, thanks. We piled into a mini-van with our fourteen boxes, pram, capsule seat, portacot, suitcases and children, who we just couldn't wake up, slobbering on our shoulders. Another stranger was wheeling Pia in the pram. Perhaps our impromptu Bangkok holiday would not be as bad as we'd first envisaged. The hotel was nice and it had a pool.

Fast forward to our arrival in London. As the plane touched down, Jason revealed that he actually didn't get his visa sorted. He didn't want to tell me before as I'd been stressed and busy and he didn't want to burden me with anything else. So he thought that moment should be the one to reveal that he'd forgotten to include critical documents such as our marriage certificate and my passport to prove he was legitimately the spouse of a European national. Luckily, it was midnight in London and there were virtually no immigration personnel and they were tired. So they stamped our passports for entry for two months, giving Jason time to get his act together.

It was 1 am when we piled into two taxis and I found the scrunched-up bit of paper with instructions about our serviced apartment, and discovered it said to collect the keys between 9 am and 4 pm. There wasn't a phone number so we proceeded to the address, convinced there'd be a note or a key.

Nope. I called Sydney and talked to my friend, Mr International. An hour and 180 quid later, we got out of our cab. It was 3 am when we finally got into our serviced apartment. It was on the fourth floor of a beautiful old building. And when I say 'old', I mean no lift. The stairs were a near vertical climb. At one point I was carrying Pia in one arm and a heavy suitcase in another, and for a brief, sleep-deprived postnatally depressed moment I really didn't think I could make it to the top of those stairs.

That night Pia slept in one of the drawers of a tallboy. It was safe; she couldn't roll out. I didn't close the drawers. The portacot we'd carried halfway around the world and up those steep stairs was broken. We'd found a nice house to rent before we left but it was unfurnished save for the white goods, and I was a little reluctant to put Pia in the fridge. So rather than spend one more day squeezing our family of five into this tiny, one-bedroom apartment on the fourth floor with no lift that Mr International had so graciously organised for us, I did what no one should ever have to do. I spent ten of my first forty-eight hours in London in IKEA.

At that point I was craving the phone call from Sydney telling me to drop everything and go to a war zone. But alas, no. I had to battle IKEA instead. At the checkout the bill came to £6284 but I'd managed to fully furnish a five-bedroom home. We moved in. The fridge was leaking and didn't work. I put a load of washing on and flooded the laundry floor, and there was no hot water for our first two days. My two-year-old came to me weeping and said, 'Please take me back to Australia.'

Now, it turned out that Graham Chapman, of *Life of Brian* fame, used to live in this house. The landlord said not to worry about minor inconveniences, like the fridge and the washing machine and the fact that the wardrobe doors had no handles and wouldn't close. She said we should be happy to be hanging clothes in the same wardrobe used by Graham. Karl Marx is buried at the Highgate cemetery and I kept thinking how happy I'd be if the landlord joined him there.

In Britain you have to send children to school the year they turn four. I had no idea what to do, so I just enrolled Allegra in the local school where my predecessor's kids went. The fees were £24,000 a year for a four-year-old. It was a month into the year when the ABC revealed that after putting the children of the correspondent before me through that school and every other correspondent before him, my children's fees would not be paid. The ABC policy had changed and from this point on, no correspondent would have their child's school fees paid.

Now, if you've lived in London you will know that public schools are a postcode lottery where waiting lists for those with reasonable academic and social records are hugely oversubscribed. But perhaps it was best. That school was posh and we had to drive. We bought a clapped-out Toyota Tarago. The parents at the school used to spend their weekends wearing tweed coats and going pigeon shooting. We were riff raff. Geraldine, the principal, required children at the age of two or three to wear a blazer, hat and tie and to shake her hand every morning with fixed eye contact and a greeting. One day, when Jason arrived to drop Allegra off, Ms Geraldine collared him and issued a firm edict for him not to park near the school anymore as our car was too noisy.

Operation Allegra quickly kicked in. Its mission: to get our daughter into the good local free school with a waiting list of 356 kids. Jason went about making regular batches of his specialty, rocky road, and he would march it up to the ladies in the office, taking the adorably cute six-month-old Pia with him for added effect. Once there he would offer around the sweets, find out our progress on the waiting list and do what he does best, which is to flirt with abandon. It worked and within a year Allegra was whisked out of the pretty private prep college where the school dresses were embossed with little flowers.

A few weeks into our stay, our air freight arrived and we were so excited. But our thrill turned to dread when we saw the first container with the familiar sticker: *Sydney storage*. It was fabulous to have a step ladder, garden tools, all our photo albums and boxes of memorabilia, such as dance trophies and soccer ribbons, and all the other stuff we didn't need in London. But that was the good news. The packers also included two of our garbage bins full of garbage. There is nothing like months' old Sydney garbage to make you feel at home.

We put the garbage out and took a brief holiday in Italy before my first assignment. That was all great until we returned to Heathrow and were forced to go through a fight at immigration as Jason still didn't have his visa. This time it took longer because now they were angry. How did Jason have the temerity to leave the country before getting his visa sorted? They held him for two hours, threatening to deport him to Australia and leave me with the three kids. Finally, they let him in and the next day he schlepped to the UK border agency in Croydon.

My first story was in beautiful Dubrovnik. It was the height of summer and, apart from a couple of stories and radio interviews, we journos spent a lot of time waiting for things to happen, sitting around the hotel pool drinking beer. I couldn't have been further away from Jason, the two babies still in nappies and the dramas at the school gate. On about day three of the gruelling Croatian schedule, I received a text from Jason. It was just four words, all in upper case: ALL THREE HAVE NITS. I glanced at the text, picked up my bottle of Peroni and took a swig.

That's my catastrophe – it's nearly ten years to the day since I was posted to London. I want to pay tribute to all the other mother correspondents, Zoe Daniel, Mary Gearin, Barbara Miller and Sophie McNeil, Sophie having won a gazillion Walkleys while being the Middle East correspondent, and she has two toddlers. Bravo!

The Smashed Avocado Catastrophe

Bernard Salt

E VER BEEN CAUGHT in a maelstrom of social media outrage? I have, and all because of a single paragraph within a single column that I had written in *The Australian Weekend Magazine* mentioning the term 'smashed avocado'. You know the issue. Every Australian knows the issue. The term 'smashed avocado' has entered both the vernacular and Australian folklore. It has come to symbolise intergenerational tensions and spending priorities.

It's a bit like the phrase that John Lennon used in 1968 at the age of twenty-eight: 'Don't trust anyone over thirty.' Lennon's advice was to the then young baby-boomer generation, even though Lennon himself was born prior to the postwar baby boom. It came to symbolise one of the key issues of the sixties and seventies, the intergenerational battle between the young and the old (defincd as anyone aged thirty-one and over).

It would appear that every generation or so, there is a market for someone somewhere to say something that ignites and/or inflames simmering intergenerational tensions. Apparently, talking about 'smashed avocado' in a column was all the incendiary that was required to cause this generation's intergenerational and indeed global outrage. The reverberations of which – rather like the 1883 explosion of the Indonesian island of Krakatoa – may still be heard thousands of kilometres from the site and the time of the original eruption.

Let me tell you how this particular catastrophe unfolded.

I am a business consultant by profession. I have written weekly columns for *The Australian* newspaper since 2002. Over the years, my columns – specialising in quirky and wry observations of social behaviour – have gathered quite a following. One of my favourite topics is the ageing of the baby-boomer generation, as that is, after all, my tribe. One of my columns, for example, talked about the game baby boomers play in social chitchat situations where they try to one-up each other with how successful and 'global' their kids are.

'My son's based in London. Not sure what he does. Something to do with high finance. Flies all over the place. Earns a squillion.'

'Really? My daughter's based in New York. She'd love to come back to Australia but there's nothing for her here.'

Nicely played on both counts. I especially like the New York riposte, which projects the idea that this baby boomer has been so successful as a parent that they have catapulted their daughter somewhere far more important than Australia.

Do you see now how skilfully the game can be played?

I had been out to lunch at a hipster restaurant in Melbourne with another person my age, and what struck me at the time, as indeed it always strikes me in these situations, was not so much the fact that the cafe's clientele invariably comprised young people (say under the age of thirty-five), but that the hushed boomer conversation centred on 'How do young people afford to eat out?'

The amusing aspect, I thought, wasn't so much that boomers were hanging out in hipster hotspots, although that in itself was column-worthy (older people 'clinging on to youth'), but rather the moralising by the middle aged about the behaviour of youth. 'Tis an issue that has been the stuff of intergenerational tension since the time of Plato.

In that instant I thought it would make a great column. I'd describe the way baby boomers quietly complain to each other about how they can't read the menu because the writing is too small. They complain that they can't hear each other speak because the music is too loud. And, of course, they can't sit on milk crates because that means their bottom is lower than their knees and they can't get back up again. And then they whisper to each other – because you could never say this out loud – 'Look at all these young people eating smashed avocado. Shouldn't they be saving for a house?' I thought this would be a marvellous parody of the kind of middle-aged moralising that has beset humanity for millennia. There is a kind of post-conceptualising calm that envelops a columnist once a column has been vigorously conceived; I felt that glow before I'd even written the piece.

The column was published on Saturday, 15 October 2016, about six months after I had started writing for the magazine. I don't think the audience quite knew my sense of humour; that I write satirically at times. There was nothing unusual about the online response to my column on the Saturday or the Sunday. It was an amusing column about baby boomers, I thought.

And then it happened.

At 6.27 am on Monday a news organisation – I don't think it was being malicious – tweeted that on the weekend Bernard Salt said that he had seen young people eating smashed avocado … shouldn't they be saving for a house. Thoughts?

I saw the tweet go live and at the time I thought, 'That doesn't look good.'

Within three hours I was fielding calls from the BBC in London. This thing went global, viral and feral almost immediately. There was no link in the tweet to the original piece. Apparently, people read a tweet and take it as a full and correct encapsulation of someone's position. No need to read the article. All the evidence that is required for a conviction and a condemnation is contained within that tweet.

By mid-afternoon 'smashed avocado' and 'Bernard Salt' were trending on Twitter. The comedian Wil Anderson was making comments; I thought they were witty. Others jumped on board; it was escalating, and I knew that this wasn't going to blow over any time soon. There were abusive direct messages. Someone from South Africa sent me a message, 'You are a …', which prompted me to learn, quickly, how to block on Twitter. I'd had no occasion to learn that function previously.

Now social media really jumped on board or 'piled on', I think, is the more correct term. A lot of it was very funny. I especially liked a two-panel meme that was up within a day: 'I stopped eating smashed avocado [picture of a smashed avocado with a diagonal line through it] … and now I own a castle.' With a picture of a fairy-tale castle replete with turrets.

The comedians at SBS developed a parody version of Kevin McCloud's *Grand Designs*, showing how to build a model house out of toast and avocado. By the end of the week 'smashed avocado' was quoted in the Australian parliament; it was used as a metaphor for the housing affordability crisis. I spoke with my boss at the consulting firm where I was a partner, and informed him of what was unfolding. The firm was very good, very supportive.

My family was upset at some of the more abusive online comments directed at me personally, but I held a more sanguine view of the whole smashed-avo catastrophe. I thought, perhaps naively, well, these people heaping abuse on me will be horribly embarrassed once they read the full column and realise that they have misinterpreted its pitch and its target (baby boomers).

Here are some of the learnings I took from the experience. There was nothing in that column that I would have written differently. Social media generally, and Twitter in particular, can 'verbal' a subject, meaning that it can restate an attributed position, and escalation and condemnation follow from there. Then again, I figured that I had been writing close to 100,000 published words every year since 2002, and so perhaps being caught in a media storm was only ever a matter of time.

I knew not to inflame the situation; not to add commentary that could be misconstrued or maliciously used to further the case against me. And then I realised how this looked from outside my bubble: I am a middle-aged male from the corporate world writing in what is perceived to be a right-leaning newspaper. I was a scalp worthy of pursuit, apparently.

Although, to be fair, I reckon that any magazine column that opens with, *Shhhh. Come close to the page. I don't want anyone to overhear what I want to talk about* – as mine did – isn't being serious. The issue is that those outraged by my comments hadn't read the column. They relied upon a Twitter summation, and then they proceeded, forthwith and happily, to anger and to condemnation.

On the following Saturday, 22 October, I wrote an explanatory piece in *The Australian*. I said that my magazine column was written as a parody of middle age – it was even entitled 'Middle-aged moralisers' – and that this parody was evident with any full and fair reading of the original piece. I politely suggested to the Twitterati that while I understood their outrage, the target of my column wasn't young people but rather middle-aged, moralising baby boomers. Online responses ridiculed my counter-argument; they said, 'So, *The Australian* is now *The Onion* … who knew,' or words to that effect.

I think there is a lesson in this for us all: make sure you have read or fully understand a person's position before proceeding to conviction. In the Twitter commentary that followed my explanation I saw one person write, *Oh, I hadn't read the actual column … I can now see that I got that wrong. Sorry.* The way social media works is that no one or very few people are accountable.

There is another observation that I have made following this experience. It is that, once you're caught on the wrong side of a social media storm, anyone who has ever hated you or merely disliked you, or has been envious of you professionally, will find that storm and gleefully enter the fray. And then when it all dies away, these adversaries will slink back into the shadows, biding their time, waiting to emerge again whenever they think you might be mortally wounded. Such is human nature, I suppose.

About a year later, the Australian *60 Minutes* program ran a story on the housing market and interviewed a thirty-something property developer, who made comments about young people's spending priorities. A link was drawn with the then still incendiary term 'smashed avocado'. That interview was picked up by the American *60 Minutes* and the whole avocado issue reverberated throughout the US. Americans today will talk of the 'Avocado Toast generation'.

I should have trademarked the term. I should have commandeered the web address smashedavo.com.au, which within a week someone had offered to sell to me. My generous offer of $22 still stands.

I think I got through this experience lightly. There was a misunderstanding of what I was saying. I was harshly criticised, but not badly and not over a sustained period. Today, the Australian people have embraced all things relating to smashed avocado. I now include a story about the column in my corporate presentations. Audiences all over Australia love it. I have suggested that we make smashed avocado the Australian national dish.

Every week I receive emails and social media links with any form of avocado paraphernalia. I have been given avocado socks, an avocado pillow case, an avocado tie, avocado Christmas decorations, and hampers of avocado and bottled feta. I have been made aware that there is an Avocado Street in Mildura where some houses are (or were) affordably priced at less than $200,000. I now know that there is a suburb in Los Angeles called Avocado.

In 2018, I received an anonymous photo of a defaced road sign 13 kilometres from the Victorian township of Avoca. Graffitists had been at work. They amended Avoca to Avocado. They added the word 'smashed'. And they put a $ sign in front of the number 13. Thus, the amended road sign read 'Smashed Avocado $13'. I immediately forwarded

the photo to *The Australian*, which promptly published both the photo and a story about the Australian penchant for amending official signs. I suggested to VicRoads that they leave it there as a tourist attraction. Sadly, VicRoads did not agree and the sign was replaced. There is a World Avocado Conference held every second year in Bogota, Colombia. I approached the organisers with an offer to

speak at the next event so that I could tell my avocado story, but they seemed very confused as to who I was and what my 'avocado research paper' might be.

Apparently, at the time of the column, my name and 'smashed avocado' made page 3 of a Stuttgart newspaper in Germany and the newspapers in Caracas, Venezuela. I know that smashed avocado was debated in London and that it made the media in Hong Kong, Dubai, Dublin and Auckland. In the middle of it all, I was contacted by a laconic wheat farmer from Western Australia who asked, 'Do you think you could do for wheat what you've done for avocados?'

And so, more than two years later, what has been the fallout? I am now mightily cautious of Twitter; it's not so much what you say as how what you say might be used against you. In many ways I am grateful for the smashed-avocado catastrophe, even though it was painful at the time. There is a fatigue factor in speaking and writing regularly: audiences get to know your shtick. Smashed avocado super-charged my profile and career at a time in life when I might otherwise have just wafted off into retirement.

Actually, I was never going to waft off into retirement. I enjoy writing and speaking and engaging with the Australian people, whom I regard as being fundamentally fair-minded. I think most Australians – even outraged Millennials – liked the whole smashed-avocado catastrophe. It highlighted the issue of housing affordability and showcased a modern-day and much-loved social behaviour – the experience of eating smashed avocado with crumbled feta on five-grain toast in an al fresco cafe.

Somehow, I don't think the Australian people are going to let go of their outrageous smashed-avocado indulgence any time soon.

Part 3

Travel Trauma

Curry in a Flurry

Jeremy Fernandez

THERE'S A VERY particular tradition in my family, which I trace back to my late paternal grandparents, Betty and Cyril Fernandez. It concerns our collective love of food.

Grandma and Grandpa were born in Kerala in South India, in the late 1920s and early 1930s, into low-to-middle-class families with big aspirations. The single greatest pillar of their upbringing was the belief in advancement through education. It was instilled in them at a young age that initiative and study were the keys to giving the next generation a better life. It was one of the reasons why they moved to Malaysia as young adults – to search for better opportunities in work and education for themselves and their children.

Betty and Cyril were both intrepid, enterprising and hardworking. In the early days, they lived in a two-bedroom wooden cottage with their eight kids. Grandpa had a job as a truck driver for the British Army, and Grandma would sell Tupperware to earn some cash.

By the time they retired, Grandpa had served as the private secretary to the Malaysian king. He and Grandma had built a beautiful home, acquired material comforts, educated their children, earned the respect of their community, and had the capacity to help others less fortunate. Like so many migrant families, one of the ways they expressed love and prosperity was through food. Food was everywhere. That's because over time, it had become easier to put food on the table. That's why food explains a big part of my family's identity.

My parents migrated from Malaysia to Perth in the 1990s, with my two sisters and me in tow. And though I now live in Sydney, I see them in Perth regularly. Every time I greet them, I can reliably predict the first three things they'll say to me:

1. Hello
2. How was your flight?
3. Are you hungry?

Without fail comes this inquiry about whether I might be famished.

Sometimes Dad will ask, 'Did you eat anything on the plane?', and I'm often too embarrassed to answer because I can sense his perfectly legitimate pity and disdain when I'd tell him about the overcooked eggs and rubbery sausages, served in a sweaty cardboard box. But I needn't worry, because there's always a freshly cooked banquet laid out at Mum and Dad's house.

Just like my grandparents, my parents' home is well stocked with food: jars of biscuits and preserved fruit, chocolates, fresh fruit and herbs from the garden, spicy Indian crisps such as pappadums and muruku. There are claypots full of curry, casserole dishes of Dad's bolognaise sauce – with a suspicious hint of Indian spices (we jokingly call it curry pasta). In fact, in some rooms in their house you don't have to reach more than about 2.5 metres to find something to eat. If a flash of hunger were to overcome you, your survival in this house would be guaranteed. You could just close your eyes, reach out in any direction, and something would inevitably fall into your hands, if not directly into your mouth.

I'm not a bad cook. I've got a few minor specialties. Despite that, I am by far the worst cook in my family. My mum, dad, sisters, and brothers-in-law are all outstanding in the kitchen – joyful, intrepid and effortless cooks. I, on the other hand, take about five hours to make a curry, by which time I've usually lost my appetite and need to lie down. So, my parents very kindly try to compensate for my relative lack of culinary expertise by sending specially made 'care packs' home with me, whenever my visit with them is over.

At first, these were small, freshly cooked and frozen bundles of my favourite meals: beef rendang, bean and mince casserole, lamb curry – all carefully wrapped and insulated in cling wrap, paper, foil, and string, ready for the flight back to Sydney. It took me a while to get used to taking food from Mum and Dad's fridges (yes, fridges). But I also came to accept that it was easier than trying to explain why I wouldn't. And truthfully, these little takeaway packs are a lifesaver. They're a taste of home, they're easy, and they spare me the effort and frustration of trying to cook something appetising for myself. Everyone I know is deeply envious and relishes the prospect of an invitation to join me for a freshly defrosted pack of curry.

Over time, these care packs have grown in number and variety. During one of my recent trips to Perth, Mum and Dad had again packed some parcels of food for me to take home. These were not small containers. Each one held about three to four servings. We were rushing to leave for the airport when Mum asked, 'Have you taken the food?'

'Oh, I forgot!' I replied. 'It's too late. I've got to leave now.'

'No,' Mum said, 'Dad has cooked it especially for you. Don't you want it?'

'Oh, all right,' I said.

She reached into the freezer and pulled out one … two … three takeaway packs.

I was feeling impatient, embarrassed, and also delighted. Mindful I was in danger of missing my flight, I also wondered how much more there was to come as she reached into the freezer again. Four … five … six … seven care packs!

Heavens!

I quickly hurled the frozen curries into my suitcase, said thank you, and ran out the door.

I arrived at the airport a little flustered, but on time. I checked in my suitcase, and raced towards the gate. I arrived at the baggage screening area, removed my laptop from my bag, took my belt off and sent it down the conveyor belt.

I stepped through the metal detector. No problems there. Then, I saw my bag on the screening monitor; it was stopped deep inside the scanning machine. The security officer gestured to a colleague, who turned to me and said, 'Sir, we're just going to put your bag through the machine again.' At this point I felt a sense of dread wash over me, and I quietly wondered, Oh no. How am I going to explain this?

To help you appraise my anxiety, I need to take you back to the house an hour earlier. After I'd hastily tucked the frozen curries into my suitcase, I was racing towards the front door when Mum said, 'What about the chicken?'

Fully aware that I already had the beef, lamb, pork and beans in my suitcase, I turned to her and asked, 'What chicken?'

'The chicken,' she said, pulling out a whole roasted chicken from the freezer. A *whole* chicken!

Baffled, and nervous about missing my flight, I said, 'Mum, I'm not taking the chicken! I'm not flying a roast chicken with me to the other side of the country.'

She couldn't understand my concern.

'Mum,' I said. 'We've got chickens in Sydney. In the shops. I don't even need to catch them. I'll be fine!'

She persisted. 'Dad made this for you. It's all packed and ready to go. It's yours. Why wouldn't you take it?'

I capitulated, and gratefully took the chicken. But because my suitcase was already full, the chicken had to go into my hand luggage.

So there we were, at the airport. As I watched my bag do a second round of the screening machine, I wondered how I was going to explain the small carcass splayed inside my bag. It also suddenly occurred to me that I might be breaking quarantine laws by attempting to transport this chicken across borders, so I agonised about the prospect of unintentionally starring in an episode of *Border Security*. It was also no help that this roast chicken was generously wrapped in foil, so it looked as if I was carrying a cannonball in my bag.

'Sir, could you open your bag. Tell me, what is this?'

'Yes, well … that's a chicken,' I mutter quietly.

'A chicken, sir?'

'Well, yes. But it's roasted. It's not alive.' I felt overcome with embarrassment, and the simultaneous urge to burst out laughing.

While all this was taking place, a steady stream of people passed through the metal detectors and overheard this exchange. A few of them had a familiar look in their eye. As someone who works on ABC television, I know this look well. They were surveying me, and thinking, I know you. You're the one. You're that … that guy from … SBS! And all I could think to say in response was, 'Hello, yes, I'm Anton Enus from SBS. Nice to meet you. Have a pleasant flight. Goodbye.'

As the security officer continued to scrutinise my chicken and the other contents of my bag, I comforted myself with the thought that she must see many strange things, and that my chicken must surely be relatively inoffensive.

After a brief but tense exchange, she let me go with my roast chicken. Victory for the chicken and me. I tucked the roast back into my bag and ran towards my departure gate, putting on my sunnies and pulling my beanie low over my face to anonymise my humiliation, but inadvertently I appeared like the wildlife smuggler I just swore I wasn't.

I'm pleased to report that after nearly five hours in the air, the chicken made it to Sydney, intact and still frozen solid. My fellow passengers were none the wiser.

I caught the train home, and just as we pulled out of Central Station, I reflected on my journey. I always miss Mum and Dad. They're generous and very good to me. I marvelled how, in a matter of a few hours, I could travel 3300 kilometres from their home to mine, on the other side of the country, with meals cooked from recipes I can trace all the way back to India. I closed my eyes, and could picture my parents, hear them, and smell the aromas of their kitchen. In fact, at that very moment, I could specifically smell lamb curry.

I opened my eyes and there, pooling at my feet, a slow drip, drip, drip of defrosting curry gravy, leaking out of my suitcase. In my haste to leave Mum and Dad's house, I decided to forego wrapping and insulating these care packs. I hadn't bothered because the curries usually make the journey so well that I thought even without the copious amounts of wrapping, she'll be right.

Well mate, she wasn't.

When I got home, I opened by suitcase to find my clothes and toiletries marinating in melting curry. 'Well! This. Is. A. Catastrophe,' I said to myself, as I slumped onto the floor. 'It's a first-world catastrophe, but it's still a catastrophe.'

But here's the thing about catastrophes such as this: if my grandparents could see how their children cook curries using the family recipes, and send these tasty parcels flying across Australia on a marvellous jetliner, with a ticket their grandson had bought himself, only to tell the tale in a book – they would call it the very opposite of a catastrophe. They would say, 'This is what we worked so hard for. We are so very proud of all of you. But ... are you hungry?'

Out Cold in Hot Japan

Deborah Knight

OLIDAYS SEEM LIKE such a good idea at the time. Tired from work – tick. Spend time with your loved ones – tick. Time to relax and reset – tick.

Except when you have three young kids like I have, who are eight, seven and one. The first mistake is to put children under five on a plane for more than fifteen minutes, and it goes downhill from there. Our holidays are a long way from the cocktails and sunsets you see on some people's Instagram feeds. Actually, I think we need to be far more realistic about what holiday snaps we post on Instagram. Let's embrace the catastrophe of travel on social media. Yes, when it comes to family holidays, we have had catastrophes in spades.

There was a particularly memorable holiday a few years ago with our two kids – aged two and three at that stage – to Japan.

I was a bit naughty and decided to fudge it with our two-year-old so we could have access to a bassinet on the flight. I said she was shorter and younger than she actually was. We had to jam her in to the bassinet, knees up, head poking out. When they were delivering the meals, the flight attendants looked at me with absolute contempt. But we got her in there, just, and had a reprieve from nursing her on our laps.

When you arrive in a foreign country with young children – well, that's an excellent life choice too – you are totally out of your comfort zone. We prised our two-year-old out of the bassinet and disembarked, arriving in Tokyo in the peak of summer. We can cope with that, we thought. After all, we cope with Sydney in summer.

We were immediately assaulted by the heat. It was intense.

We thought we'd take the train from Narita airport into Tokyo with the kids and all the baggage. Yes, all the baggage. Five large suitcases in total. Because for some reason I thought that instead of buying nappies when we got there, I should bring them all with me, three weeks' worth in the suitcase. Also, rather than purchase snacks in Japan, I would bring three weeks' worth with me because, heaven forbid, what if one of the kids couldn't eat their organic, free-range sultanas while on holiday? Got to protect that delicate Australian palate.

There we were, walking along with our five suitcases stacked and teetering on a luggage trolley, when we were confronted by a row of bollards in our way. We had to pull the luggage off while carrying the kids with us. Next, because the heat was so intense, we decided that before catching the train, we should change the kids out of the clothes they were wearing. The only problem was that we couldn't see a place to change them, so we did it right there on the concourse at the train station, with people all around us.

Eventually, while we were trying to get all the luggage together and plan our next move, the kids started playing that game kids love to play – running around in circles and laughing. It was all good until the younger one tripped, fell hard, hit her head and was knocked unconscious. Out. Cold.

What should we do?

My husband had some basic language skills picked up years ago while travelling through Japan for about three weeks. But I suspected he hadn't mastered the phrase 'My toddler has a concussion.' Nevertheless, he took off with the limp child in his arms to try to find some help.

I stood there, surrounded by luggage, holding the hand of my conscious child, wondering how I was going to find out where he had gone. Neither of us had a working phone.

After a while he returned with our daughter in his arms, screaming. It was one of those times when crying is the best sound in the world. So, we thought, she's okay and alert. If she fell unconscious again we'd head to a hospital, but until then we would barrel on.

At last, we arrived in Tokyo. It was our first time using Airbnb and we thought we were hip and groovy. But the quaint apartment we were staying in, which looked so good in the photographs, was actually adjacent to a major construction site. The buildings in Japan have to be earthquake-proof, and the workers were doing the kind of foundation-shaking construction required by local building codes from dawn to dusk the entire time we were there. Also, we could smell a raw cabbage stench coming from the immense, deep hole they were digging into the earth.

The three-year-old was in heaven – he loved the diggers and bulldozers and trucks – but we decided we couldn't stay there a moment longer and so we found a serviced apartment.

Overall it was a great holiday and we had a great time. The Japanese are incredibly polite and helpful, especially with children. They would give us quizzical looks as we squeezed onto the train in the Tokyo summer heat at peak hour, my husband with a backpack, me with the stroller and all the stuff you need when you travel with kids – bags and toys galore – and the two children. They thought we were insane.

They were even nice when we lost things, which happened a lot. My son had a red car, a Lightning McQueen from the movie *Cars*, which he lost in an enormous food hall. We enlisted about ten staff to find his beloved car. It took us over two hours but we found it. As we left the food hall we walked past a gigantic toy store with an elaborate window display with about a thousand toy cars exactly the same as the one we had been searching for all that time.

The final catastrophic moment of the trip: we'd finished dinner at a restaurant and we were close to end of my three-week stash of nappies, so my husband went off to buy some more. I was preoccupied with my two-year-old when I looked around and realised the three-year-old was gone. No longer in the restaurant. I rushed to the door and looked out to a scene of Kyoto at peak hour, a sea of people. That's it, I thought, I'll never see him again.

I grabbed a chair from the restaurant and stood on it. I thought I might see his blond bobbing head in the throng.

Sure enough, coming through the crowd, holding the hands of two smiling people, there he was, having a great time, calm as could be.

I am now a huge fan of writing my phone number on my children's arms, even though they roll their eyes at me when I do. If we're going to the Easter Show, out comes the felt-tip pen.

When it comes to holidays, they aren't relaxing, but they are life-affirming, bonding experiences where you get to observe how your partner copes under pressure.

I hope to take the kids to Japan again someday, without the nappies and the sultanas but with a phrase book of essential medical terms, just in case.

A Greek Tragedy ...
Or why you should never give up until the final siren sounds

Wendy Harmer

HAULING YOUR SORRY, dumped arse to a comedy festival seems like the perfect way to mend a broken heart. Especially if it's as far away as Scotland and you can put almost 17,000 kilometres and two continents between you and the dreaded ex.

The Edinburgh Festival Fringe is just the ticket for what ails a lovelorn Aussie lassie.

Thousands of funny shows to choose from that have you crying with laughter in the anonymous dark. Drinking the bars dry with lovely, red-headed Scottish boys. Wandering deserted cobblestone streets in the witching hours, serenaded by pissed caterwauling bagpipers belting out 'Loch Lomond'.

With a few wee drams under the belt it's easy to cast yourself as Aggie, poor servant girl turned out from Inverary Castle by the wicked Duke of Argyll. Starring in one's own tragic historical drama is sure to bring on a bout of epic, ugly crying. Very therapeutic.

At dawn, breakfast is taken on the bluestone steps of a bakery. Beef and onion bridies with brown sauce – sauce so named because it has no other characteristic. It's *nae* hot, it's *nae* spicy. It's just *brun*. Stumbling into your shared digs, stepping over suitcases, falling into bed and sleeping, dreamlessly, till late afternoon. Then doing it all again the next day and night.

Three solid weeks of this punishing regime should see any broken heart out of ICU and on the road to recovery.

Och, aye!

However, it's an entirely different matter if you're going to the festival to bring the laughs as a stand-up comedian, hideously cursed with knowing all the maudlin lyrics to 'The Bonnie Banks O' Loch Lomond'.

> *O ye'll tak' the high road, and I'll tak' the low road,*
> *And I'll be in Scotland a'fore ye,*
> *But me and my true love will never meet again,*
> *On the bonnie, bonnie banks o' Loch Lomond.*

> *'Twas there that we parted, in yon shady glen,*
> *On the steep, steep side o' <u>Ben Lomond,</u>*
> *Where in soft purple hue, the hieland hills we view,*
> *And the moon coming out in the gleaming.*

———

The Edinburgh Fringe Festival was where I found myself in the early nineties, bereft and broken-hearted. I'd been to the festival before, in shows with other comics, and one year I went with *him*. But this time, the airfares and accommodation were just for me after the Mother of All Break Ups.

(A tip. Never ask the question: 'Don't you love me anymore?' unless you're prepared for the answer to be a tight-lipped, 'No.')

That year, my world in Melbourne had shrunk to a few blocks around St Kilda's Acland Street and the band room at the Esplanade Hotel I haunted as a forlorn, hard-drinking ghost of my former self. I couldn't face driving north over the Punt Road Bridge in case I ran into *them*. My old haunts of Fitzroy, Collingwood and Richmond, home of the mighty Tigers, my Aussie Rules footy team, were out of bounds.

One time I'd crossed the Yarra, saw *them* and quickly retreated across the bridge to my small flat near the beach. Or should I say, *our* old flat where every meal for one – usually a Salada biscuit with Vegemite and cheese and a bottle of Shiraz – was taken like a penance. To describe myself as miserable doesn't go close. I was a shambling, cried-out, puffy-eyed wreck of a woman.

With a few gigs booked, television interviews and radio spots already scheduled at The Fringe, it seemed as good an escape plan as any. So, packing a suitcase with a few shards of broken heart, some half-decent jokes and a tiny scrap of self-esteem in a toiletries bag, I headed to Edinburgh.

Just me this time. Taking the low road to Scotland.

Fetching up in Edinburgh that late August, I'd booked into an upscale hotel just off the main drag in Princes Street. In the past I'd shared rowdy, crowded flats with other comics and *him*, but this time I figured the luxurious solitude would be a comfort. (A mistake, obviously.)

That wasn't the only difference to my past forays at The Fringe. Instead of presenting a full show with fellow comedians in the one venue at the decent hour of 8 or 10 pm, this time I'd put together a grab bag of solo stand-up gigs and MC work in the clubs that only got going at midnight and stayed open until the heaving small hours. That meant I'd have to stay sober all evening and by the time I got off stage, my usual posse of drinking mates were ready for bed. (Second mistake, even more obvious.)

The grey days were spent alone, visiting glorious national monuments in the drizzling rain and wondering if various stone castle parapets were high enough to jump off. The early evenings were spent in the bath, cursing the groaning Scottish plumbing and tepid water. Still, I managed to keep myself nice and the gigs went well. So well that I'd picked up a solid timetable of extra bookings for the full three weeks.

By the end of week two, I was in the full grip of SCS (Sad Clown Syndrome). Much of my stand-up routine was about being single well into my thirties – a litany of romantic failures that got the big laughs. But the more they laughed, the worse it was for me. With a four-day gap in my diary, what I needed was an escape from my escape.

The Brits call them 'mini-breaks' and it was the Greek island of Crete that took my eye. Less than a hundred pounds for four nights in a villa on the beach just outside the capital, Heraklion. Sun, sand, azure waters.

Yoghurt and honey for breakfast. Fresh salads with olives and feta for lunch. Slow-roasted lamb for dinner. A day trip to the famed Palace of Knossos. Shopping for blue and white ceramic treasures.

Sold!

If this didn't lift my spirits, my next escape would see me off to the Arctic Circle.

The logistics of getting to Crete from Edinburgh and back in time for my next gig were ... let's say *challenging*. The worst leg would be the flight from Gatwick, which left at the god-forsaken hour of 4 am for the four-hour trip.

That I remember the ordeal of that flight some thirty years later is a testament to how truly horrendous it was – delayed for hours and packed to the gunnels with English tour groups that had been drinking solidly since last Thursday.

I'm not gunna talk their shit foreign language, or eat their crap food. Forget it. If I don't get a full English ... wif proper chips ... I'm comin' home, me!

Four hours of chucked beer cans, duty-free vodka passed down the aisles, and pub sing-a-longs saw me in the foetal position. And, predictably, I was coming down with a middle-ear infection. My poor ears have always been my Achilles heel when I'm run down. I'm afflicted with thundering headaches, nausea and dizziness – especially when flying. The descent into Heraklion had me sobbing. How I got to my accommodation is a blur. But I'll never forget my first sight of that 'charming Grecian villa'.

The joint was a bomb site. Half-built. Workers swarming all over it with concrete mixers and pneumatic drills; the 'reception area' was covered with a tarpaulin; half the 'dining room' was knee-deep in rubble. The two guest rooms that had been 'finished' were out the back – just bare concrete boxes with wires sticking out of the walls.

Too weak to protest, and by now running a galloping fever from the roaring inflammation in both ears, I collapsed into bed and spent the next forty-something hours in a delirium, wincing with every hammer blow and bone-shattering drill. Only shouts of '*Kalimera*' or '*Kalispera*' signalled that day was passing into night.

I wept for my sorry self, and wondered if anyone knew where I was, or if they cared. Except that, when all was quiet and still in the evening, I could draw the curtain on the window by my bed and see the hills and mountains. Lights twinkled up there, away in the darkness, and I longed to be spirited there, to spend a night looking out to the peaceful Sea of Crete and the endless wonders of the Aegean.

Perhaps I wasn't fully conscious of it then … but a plan was forming.

With the departure from my Greek idyll looming fast and not one toe even dipped in the 'azure' waters, I rallied to totter over the main road to the beach that last, late afternoon, barely avoiding being skittled by tattooed Brit backpackers on speeding motorbikes.

Oi, watch where yer goin', ya dozy bint!

A desultory stretch of sand awaited – not even as nice as St Kilda – and crowded with lithe, tanned, topless Dutch, Danish and German backpackers thumping volleyballs and furiously shouting … names of cheese?

Gouda. Havarti. Klemensker. Edam!

I trudged back to the bomb site, packed my bag, and left it in the foyer for the morning bus.

As the warm night descended, I asked for a taxi.

'Take me there,' I said to the driver, pointing to the lights in the mountains.

'Where?' Without a name for the destination he was puzzled.

'Just up there.' I pointed again to a string of pink tinsel glinting in the dusky sunset.

Up and up the narrow winding road we went. On one side the hillside fell away into woody ravines and beyond that the magnificent Sea of Crete. The driver slowed on a bend to trail an elderly fellow walking the road ahead, shepherding his flock of goats and sheep, each one with a tinkling tiny bell strung around its neck. I hadn't heard such a soothing sound in, what seemed like, forever. Exactly what I'd been seeking to balm my savage soul.

I got out and watched the taxi's tail lights disappear back down the mountain. On wobbly legs I followed the shepherd to the small village just ahead.

The heady scent of rosemary and lemon led me to a roadside kitchen where a few locals sat on the balcony. Without much Greek, except for a grateful '*Evcharisto poli*', a feast magically appeared of delicious olives, feta, slow-cooked lamb (sorry, lambs) and a tumbler of rosé retsina.

Watching the sun drop below the edge of the world and with a profound, blessed quiet closing in, my equilibrium was being restored. All I needed was a bed for the night and I'd be on my way. Ready to head back to the fray.

When the kitchen closed, I walked further up the hill to where I supposed the main village must be. But no, turning back, this was it. A single street light, a handful of modest houses and all the curtains drawn. I cursed myself for being so stupid. This wasn't a proper plan. I'd fled my concrete box on a whim and hadn't thought anything through. Typical.

No matter, I decided. I'll just walk back down the mountain. And if it took all night? Then, that's what it would take. How far could it be? No more than 10 kilometres, I estimated. Maybe fifteen?

Setting off with gravel crunching underfoot and the tang of pine trees hanging in the warm night air, my spirits were high. I imagined regaling all my friends back home with my great nocturnal adventure in the forests of Crete!

A mere 100 metres or so down the road and I stopped dead. All was pitch black. No moonlight. On one side a precipitous cliff. Still dizzy and unbalanced from my illness, I could so easily stumble and plunge over the edge.

I had to turn back to the village and beg for a bed.

The first door I knocked on opened just a tiny crack and quickly slammed shut. And the one after that.

With only a few houses left it looked like I'd be spending the night on the footpath or sneaking into a pen with the sheep and goats for the warmth. It was getting chilly now and I'd only brought a fresh shirt and socks in my tote bag.

Stupid. Dumb. Me.

The next door, mercifully, was opened a little wider by a tiny, elderly lady.

'*Yassas. Kalispera*,' I gabbled.

An elaborate mime ensued that I hoped translated as: 'Please, please. Do you have a bed I could sleep in? I will pay you for your troubles. Please say yes because I am a desperate idiot and I ...'

I could see she was thinking, who is this crazy woman? as the door started to creak to a close.

'I've come from Melbourne in Australia ... I ...'

She paused then, held up one finger that I translated to mean, 'Just one moment,' and called over her shoulder.

A young man appeared in the doorway. Tall, bearded and imposing.

'You from Melbourne?' he asked. A gruff and rough inquiry.

'Yes. Melbourne.'

He paused for a long while and then asked, 'So ... what team you barrack for?'

There was only one answer. The correct answer. 'Richmond. The mighty Tigers, of course!'

He beamed from ear to ear. 'Richmond! Richmond! Tigerland! Come in! Come in! Welcome to you, friend!'

As we shared a cup of herbal tea in his family's small kitchen, the young man told me his story. He'd lived in Melbourne for some years and had only recently returned to his ancestral home in this tiny, picturesque rural village. His family was opening a B&B, just next week, as it happened. The tourist trade in Crete was booming and I certainly wasn't the first who'd come looking for a place to stay. They had only one room ready. Would I like to be their very first guest?

I said I would. Thank you very much.

His mother scurried off to make everything ready.

Just as, even now, I can vividly recall that bomb site down the mountain, the details of that wonderful room abide in my memory.

Whitewashed walls with little nooks where candles glowed. A wooden dressing table set with a blue and white ceramic jug of water with slices of lemon. Creamy, soft, flokati rugs on the floor. A big bed topped with a bright, striped woven spread. And, most magnificently, two wooden doors that opened to the vast expanse of the Cretan sea, where a thousand points of light twinkled into infinity.

As I slept that night on Mount Olympus, I could only think that Zeus Xenios – the Greek god of hospitality and travellers – had guided me there. Perhaps the son of Apollo, Asclepius, and his five famous healing daughters ministered to me in my dreams too.

I only know that upon waking to a breakfast of fresh yoghurt, honey, eggs and bread, I was restored. Ready to head down the mountain again and to all that awaited.

My very ordinary (by most standards), adventure that year often comes to mind. I can only think it's because, during my heartache, I'd limited my world to a tiny frame. Couldn't even cross the Punt Road Bridge back then. But with a scrap of courage, more than a little luck and a foolish, trusting heart, the whole world was mine again.

Many have since asked, what if you'd answered 'Collingwood' or 'St Kilda' to the young man's question?

I'll leave you to ponder that.

I never have.

PS: I did return to the Edinburgh Fringe Festival. Next time with a one-woman show called *Love Gone Wrong*, all about the travails of the broken-hearted. It was nominated 'Pick of the Fringe' and transferred for a short run in London's West End.

So there's that.

Och, aye!

The Ninja Star, the Federal Police and Me

Andrew P. Street

THERE ARE PEOPLE who see the glass as half full. There are people who see the glass as half empty. And there are people who see the glass as full of poison and about to explode in their faces.

All those people are, in my opinion, adorable optimists.

For much of my life, at least until I discovered that a small and regular dose of specific chemicals helped prevent it, my constant and overwhelming anxiety would reassure me that everything was always about to come crashing down around my ears, almost certainly because of some stupid thing that I, like an idiot, had overlooked.

For the most part, that feeling was both unhelpful and incorrect. And yet the one time it would have been absolutely on the money I was blithely standing at Adelaide airport, watching the security personnel scanning and re-scanning my bag, and inexplicably not experiencing my usual sinking feeling that things were about to go stupidly awry.

It was March 2006, and I was eager to leave Adelaide for the weekend to visit my then wife. She had just been headhunted for a project in Sydney and was being put up in Woolloomooloo by her new company until she secured accommodation. Meanwhile, I was in Adelaide trying to pack up our life. She had told me that I didn't actually need to follow her if I didn't want to leave A-town, a statement that probably should have registered a little more strongly with me than it did.

At that time, I was working as the music editor at *dB Magazine*, a free street-press magazine. Also working there a year or so earlier had been a designer named Anthony, whom we had nicknamed 'Ninja' for reasons my memory has obscured.

After leaving us and the entire badly listing South Australian publishing industry, he travelled to Japan to teach English, where he met a local girl and they fell in love. In December 2005, he brought his beloved to Australia to meet his family, and popped into the office with some fun novelty presents for each of us: ornamental ninja stars made of metal and looking entirely authentic. We all laughed at them, and I put mine into my shoulder bag and completely forgot about it.

And thus a few months later I was initially confused when a sheepish-looking security guard came over and asked a question that I'm betting he didn't often get the chance to ask. 'Excuse me, sir, but is there any reason why you would be, um, attempting to carry a throwing star on to this flight?'

I laughed. 'Of course not!' I confidently declared. 'Why on Earth would I be carrying … *Oh my dear god.*'

'Come with me, sir,' said the suddenly rather less pally security guard.

In the guard's defence, he absolutely believed my breathless story about why this object was in my bag, since it made a lot more sense than any of the alternatives. For one thing, ninjas are notoriously stealthy. The fact that I was now sitting in a small office with three members of airport security whose day had just got a lot more interesting, instead of having done a backflip into an air vent before vanishing, ghostlike, into the night, was a bit of a giveaway that I was probably more disorganised idiot than master assassin.

I did learn that the reason they were scanning and rescanning my bag was because the system occasionally threw up fake scans to ensure that the airport security guards were still paying eagle-eyed attention after days and weeks and years of zero terrorist threats in Adelaide. When the object remained after two scans, they started to take seriously the possibility that it was real and … well, there we were.

The other thing I learned was that the actual police had been informed and now we were waiting to hear if the guards had decided whether it was an honest if stupid mistake, or they wanted to interview me and check that I wasn't, in fact, a covert saboteur from feudal Japan.

At this point I was more embarrassed than worried. I'd arrived unnecessarily early for my flight, a paranoid trait connected with my aforementioned anxiety, which infuriates my travel companions to this day. I figured I'd soon be sent on my way, one ninja star down but compensated with exciting new knowledge and experience. Actually, it would be a relief: anxiety might be a hellish burden most of the time, but the wave of relief that washes over me when I realise that my fears were absolutely justified – that stuff is *intoxicating*.

Just as the guards shrugged and said I might as well go, the phone rang. Why yes, the South Australian Police told them, they would very much like to have a chat with me after all.

The looks on the faces of the guards made me aware that the shit had just got a little more real.

———

The two men from SAPOL were less impressed with my apologetic charm and goofy tales about the nicknames attributed to former colleagues. This, they stressed, was Very Serious Indeed and maybe I should call a lawyer.

Despite this sage counsel I did not, for several reasons. One was that I still hoped to catch my flight. Two was that I didn't actually have a lawyer or any clear idea of how one was found. I felt this was a point in my favour – the sorts of people that needed lawyers would immediately know how to get hold of one, and therefore my story was even *more* plausible. This, the police assured me, was incorrect on several levels.

Finally, after twenty-five minutes or so, the police were convinced that I wasn't a threat, or perhaps too dumb to be dangerous. I was told that I was free to go but might be called back for further questioning, especially if the Federal Police were intrigued.

With an agility that I now realise was perhaps a little too ninja-y I leapt to my feet, thanked them, and proceeded to race down to the concourse.

The flight was closed but the rep from the airline was certain that we could still make it provided that he yelled into an intercom and that I ran like Tom Cruise in every goddamn film of his.

And thus, with two people from the airline at my flanks, we ran like a pack of dogs were pursuing us down to the gate, where they opened the door to the about-to-disconnect airbridge and alerted the cabin crew to halt the door arming and crosschecking process.

I raced panting onto the plane to face row after row of unimpressed-looking passengers, found my seat and sat down. The doors were shut and secured. The engine revved up.

Sweating, panting, I relaxed.

And then the engines revved down again.

The doors became unarmed, un-crosschecked and un-shut in order to welcome two different uniformed police officers on board, who strode up to me, took my bag from the overhead compartment, and loudly invited me to escort them off the plane in order that we might go have a chat with the Federal Police.

This was about the point where I realised that I wasn't going to Sydney after all.

———

The feds kept me waiting for about ninety minutes before they began their chat, which was either a killer psychological trick to ensure that I was feeling thirsty and emotionally fraught, or it was a Friday and they really couldn't be arsed rushing through anything.

Either way, their line of questioning was not as warm and welcoming as that of the police. Who had given me the ninja star? What did I mean, I didn't have a contact for Anthony in Japan?

'He's a friend and you can't even name the city he's in?'

No, email wasn't good enough, they needed a number. No, I couldn't have my phone back. Why was I bringing a ninja star on a flight? Did

I expect them to believe that I'd simply forgotten? No, really, *Why was I bringing a ninja star on the flight?*

A tiny little part of me really wanted to say, 'What possible answer are you looking for? That I planned to overpower the cabin crew using a piece of costume jewellery and then force the pilots to bow to my commands, lest I poke them with the edges of the cellophane wrapping in which the thing was still sealed? That I planned to commandeer this domestic flight and demand the pilots fly me to Heian-kyō, seat of feudal power in the Heian period? How much are you fuckers getting off on this pointless exercise of power?'

Fortunately, a much, *much* larger part of me told that tiny part to shut the hell up and make this all finish, and also that maybe crying a bit would be a good idea. That might have just been because I was tired and hungry, to be honest, or maybe because I'd noticed that my wife hadn't been as fussed about my no longer coming as I might have reasonably assumed from my phone call. That could have been a foreshadowing of how the next eighteen months would shake out, had I bothered to question it.

But, hey, I wasn't about to search the deepest corners of my marriage at that point. Evidently I wasn't even in the emotional place to search the deepest corners of my carry-on luggage.

At last, after an hour of circular arguments and threats about just how bad they could make things for me, the fight abruptly went out of my interrogators and they plonked a document in front of me to sign. The gist of said document was that they would be keeping my ninja star – thereby robbing me of what would have been a hilarious prop in retellings of this story – and that I would have an active record with the Federal Police in case there was a sudden spate of ninja terrorism. The file would eventually be closed when I was deemed no longer a threat.

That period turned out to be a matter of weeks, at which point I went into the Federal Police headquarters in Adelaide's CBD and signed another bit of paper. In my memory it was a year or more later but, given that I was living in Sydney by May, that can't possibly have been the case. Also, I remember it just saying that I was not a ninja, with a helpful little cartoon of a masked figure in a circle with a line through it. But I'm pretty sure that can't be right either.

All that was to come, though. After my interrogation it was well and truly late, but I went back to the terminal to have a chat with the airline staff about how many flights remained that evening (none), how much of a refund I'd receive given the circumstances (sharp intake of breath), and how I'd feel about being rescheduled to a 6.30 flight the following morning (cautiously positive, although given the amount of wine I correctly anticipated I would be drinking over the course of the evening to come, that flight would be a turbulent journey of hungover regret worthy of its own story).

As a white middle-class man there were obviously no repercussions. I've travelled internationally with not so much as a question at Customs about my shady *Shinobi* past, and have tweeted inflammatory rhetoric about Peter Dutton without worrying that it would land me on Christmas Island.

I did remain vigilant about checking my bag for damn near everything for years afterwards, until the rules at different airports became so individual and arbitrary that I couldn't be bothered trying to remember if this specific airport had declared war on fold-up umbrellas or whether security guards would respond to my pulling out a Ventolin inhaler by staring at me as though I was mad. So I figured that I'd just push my bag through and let Fate decide.

But I do know what I'll do next time I see them scan and rescan my bag: throw down a smoke grenade and disappear like a ghost. 'You want to know about my bag? I wasn't even there, copper. *I wasn't even there.*'

Mind My Baby

Cathy Wilcox

THIS IS A story set in Paris, about a catastrophe that's arguably not huge on a world scale. It's a story of travel and how sometimes you forget to take proper account of how having a baby can affect your plans.

I was invited one year to go and stay with my long-time friend Celina, who lived in a nice suburb on the outskirts of Paris, about an hour from the centre by train. I'd known her since we were both beginners in that big city – me, a graduate Arts student and avowed Francophile looking to define myself outside the parameters of suburb, school and snobberies of Sydney; and Celina, who had fled to Paris from Poland as a political refugee, with no French, no passport and no recognition in France of her qualifications and experience as a psychologist.

We'd met through a colleague of mine at the English language magazine where I'd found work. It was a time of freedom, before either of us had responsibility for others.

We bonded later during my time there when I suffered the loss of a lover, and discovered, through her sympathetic gesture of a half-full bottle of vodka, that Celina had experienced a similar loss. She's one of my great friends in life.

Some years down the track, when I had married and had my second child, she called to say that her husband and son were off to visit the grandparents for summer, so why didn't I come to stay with her outside Paris for a few weeks with my small baby Felix? We could hang out like old times. My husband could look after our older child back home – that'd be fun for them. 'Hey, why not?'

When the words 'Hey, why not?' come out of your mouth or even pop up in your brain, you should hear alarm bells.

But anyway, it seemed like a great idea. Felix was around eight months old, a very happy, easy baby; I'd been back and forth to France many times – once with my husband and our firstborn – and I'd be staying with my great friend, who'd mothered her own child. She'd be able to mind the baby while I travelled into the city and enjoyed some 'me time' in the boutiques.

Felix was, as I say, an amenable baby, but although he was adapting to solid food he had a particularly sensitive gag reflex and couldn't tolerate lumps of any kind. Also, an avid breast-feeder – he absolutely refused to take a bottle – he tended to gorge himself until over-full. I had never had a chance to enjoy the mother–baby idyll of co-sleeping with him or his older sibling, as they'd both been prodigious chuckers and a feed in bed would always result in everyone being soaked. Still, no problems, I should be able to cook and blend simple food for him at Celina's.

The month was July. It was a cold winter in Sydney and we travelled to a warm and humid summer in Paris. You'd think that would be a good thing. The other thing about summer in Paris is that it becomes daylight very early and stays light until very late. I had a baby angel who was a great sleeper, so long as he was sleeping in a darkened room. He sucked neither thumb nor dummy – my breast was his preferred soother.

At Celina's place, the shutters on our windows were broken and there were no blinds. So when it was light, it was light. That was the first thing.

It turns out, in case you didn't know, that eight-month old babies aren't very responsive to the hands on a clock. They can't simply be told that they're in a different time zone so could they please sleep now. If we adults take a couple of days to switch zones, the best you can hope with a little kid is that they'll gradually adjust by a couple of hours a day. This meant that I was trying to be wakeful during the day, to adjust, but being on call all night for an infant who would want to play, or be attended to, or cry, or feed. Crying would wake my friend and the neighbours. So besides cuddling and comforting, feeding seemed the only thing to soothe him.

Can I mention here that the other thing about travelling from winter to summer with a baby is that the baby gets extra thirsty in the heat? I will also mention that for who-knows-what reason, dear little baby Felix didn't like the taste of Paris water, from tap or bottle. Also, he completely lost his appetite for the baby mush that was offered to him. Some of the finest quality fruit, veg and poultry were rejected. He only wanted my breast for food; he only wanted my breast for drink; and he only wanted my breast for comfort.

It's so great to be needed.

One week into my girlfriends holiday in Paris and I was getting a little run-down from sleep deprivation and my very bones were being sucked hollow by an adorable baby with a winning smile and a jaunty quiff. Oh yes, did I mention? Felix was such a great traveller that people on the Paris Metro would lose their stony grimaces and point out this little cherub to one another, so winsome was his public engagement.

These people were not spending the night with my crying baby leech monster.

As I said, Felix's tendency was to overfeed. The consequence of this, as we tried to keep quiet in the night in my friend's son's carpeted bedroom, was that, while I tried and tried to take him off the breast asleep, he would wake and demand more. Eventually he'd stop, look at me, then with a slight puff of the cheeks, spew forth the contents of his bloated stomach, covering me in a veil of warm milk. You see, I had to aim him at me, so he wouldn't vomit on the carpet.

And then we'd have a bath in our clothes.

Well, after a week or so of this, Felix was gradually adjusting to the time zone, if hardly at all to the food. I was letting go of all my usual 'healthy baby' eating rules and hoping that the mere presence of sugar or 'biscuit flavour' would persuade him to eat something that wasn't a byproduct of me. It was impossible to consider leaving him in Celina's care while I popped into town for a spot of shopping. So I figured, how hard could it be to get around Paris with Felix in his stroller?

Oh! Another thing about travelling to the northern summer from the southern winter is the food. By July I'm usually tired of apples and oranges at home, but with Celina there's always a feast. Since moving to Paris, she has taken pride and pleasure in the quality and variety of produce, and she's learned to make the very best of French cuisine.

A trip to the local produce market was something we could certainly manage, and I could savour the pleasure that comes from a bounty of cheeses, fruit and veg, charcuterie, bread and pastry. And believe me, while my cute little bloodsucker was sucking the marrow out of me, I at least had somewhere to put all that lovely food.

There was a bag full of apricots that was particularly memorable – so sweet and full of fragrance and flavour – and just on the point of overripe, so we had to eat them without delay. Yum!

So there I was, wondering how hard could it be to go into Paris for the day with Felix in the stroller.

'How hard could it be?' is a question like, 'Hey, why not?'

I had lived in Paris for nearly three years; I knew my way around pretty well and wasn't hampered by language. I also knew it wasn't always a kind city, so you have to be pretty sure of yourself.

If it has an exemplary public transport system by comparison to our own, then being young, fit and able are necessary conditions to that example, because there are obstacles all the way for the elderly, infirm or people with children. Just pushing through those magnetised doorways or the full-height turnstiles, or getting up and down the stairs is enough to challenge the hardiest sleep-deprived mother. Sometimes you'd have to talk into intercoms to get a special door opened. But occasionally, kind people would see you with your baby and stroller at the foot of a busy staircase and offer to help you. So I mustered my courage, considered my destinations and set out with Felix for a day in Paris.

My favourite place always ends up being around the Marais, north of the Hôtel de Ville, with smaller scale buildings and a mix of funky boutiques, hipster, gay and ethnic Jewish culture. Unlike Sydney, in Paris some places don't change, and you can sometimes go back and find the same waiter in the same cafe, year after year. Also, each traditional cafe is much like another, so you know what you'll find there in terms of food and conveniences. And blessedly, they've upgraded the conveniences, so you rarely have to negotiate a piddle-puddled stinking hole in the floor.

I needed a cafe for my convenience. So I ordered coffee, made chitchat with the waiter and – after little Felix had worked his usual magical charm – I entrusted him to watch my baby in the stroller while I went to the loo. Even if it's hard to get around, Paris is pretty baby friendly.

There was another area I wanted to get to, up around the Canal St Martin. It wasn't one of my regular old haunts but it was always beautiful, and I'd heard it had undergone a wave of renewal and was cool and interesting. We made our way there by Metro and went exploring the surrounds of the Canal, walking along streets I hadn't checked out before. I was yet to find the very hip and happening parts … maybe they were over the other side of the canal.

And then I felt the gripe.

A gurgling, a groaning, a clenching …

All. Those. Apricots.

I really needed a toilet.

I walked and walked and hoped to find a cafe, a shop, a something.

Did I mention that July in Paris can be very quiet? Most of the locals go on holiday, and away from the touristy areas, lots of businesses close for the summer.

Walking with Felix in his stroller, with no obvious way across the canal except maybe a bridge further along with lots of stairs (I would have burst if I'd carried the stroller up any stairs), and on this side, nothing but residential buildings with their secure entrances, or closed shops …

With my stomach growling relentlessly, I actually began to wonder if there were places – plants, walls or doorways – I could squat behind to relieve myself of this painful griping, or if my bowels were just going to make the decision for me …

Then I saw a business. A gym, with a big glass door. Please be open!

The door opened. There was a big, buff man looking bored and beautiful behind the counter. He was not like the baby-charming waiters in the cafes, and would have happily ignored us until I asked him as succinctly as possible if there was a toilet I could use, as it was an emergency. He gestured behind me – a staircase that went down about three floors. The toilet was down there, at the bottom. I looked at the stairs, then at Felix in the stroller, then at the bored man behind the counter, and my bowels groaned.

'Please mind my baby!' I said, and I ran down those stairs and truly, just made it.

It had been a tough choice, but luckily my baby was still there at the top of the stairs when I returned, cooing adorably while the muscled man studied his own perfection. I thanked him profusely and gave up on finding the groovy part of the Canal St Martin.

Nothing much else to report from that trip, except in the second week I got terrible bronchitis and went home sick. I was so run-down. Felix drained me dry on our return to Sydney because he had to adjust to the time zone again. I had to wean him, just to recover some strength. My sleep was so disrupted that I developed insomnia, during which time I had a crisis of faith and lost God, needed years of therapy and medication.

But I'm fine now. I just pause for a little longer when I think, 'Hey, why not?', and make sure I go easy on the apricots.

On a Fin and a Prayer

James Jeffrey

D EATH COMES TO us all in the end. I just didn't expect it to
come disguised as a chicken.

Barely able to see, my face apparently stuffed with pins, my
chest with knitting needles and my throat with a fist, I listened to the
rumble of the 747's jet quartet over my gasps. Beneath me, the belly of the
Korean Air jumbo bulged with suitcases in chilly darkness. Beneath that
stretched 11,000 metres of sky and cloud and air pocket. And beneath
that lay the sea from which my accidental killer had come. I pictured my
death notice: 'James Jeffrey – born prematurely, Great Britain. Died in
the same manner, row 36.' Then cursing anaphylaxis, I passed out.

My first mistake had probably been in drawing attention to myself. I'd
been planning a trip to Europe – backpacking from my father's country
in the west to my mother's in the east – when my eye was caught by the
jaunty blue fuselage of a Korean Air plane roaring out of Sydney. I had a
sudden vision: I would spend three days passing through the restaurants
of Seoul like a whale through krill, before heading to Scotland,
which – how to say this lovingly? – was less of a culinary destination
than it is now.

But my ticket wasn't going to be just any old ticket, it was going to
be *special*. Looking back, it's not clear why I did what I did. Perhaps

I mysteriously reasoned an Asian airline was more likely to serve what I'd come to view as death flesh, my own glittering, scale-armoured Kryptonite. More probably it was because I'd noticed on earlier flights that everyone on special food lists – vegan, kosher and the rest – got fed first.

'I'd like to add a dietary requirement to my booking,' I informed the travel agent, for it was the mid-1990s and we were yet to suffer the internet. 'No fish.'

And with that, my destiny was written.

That I was powerfully allergic to fish was a discovery Mum and Dad made early in my life, during a series of trial and error. It was a culinary experiment in which they tried to kill me every Friday. This was fish-and-chips night, and each time they watched in almost academic curiosity as my lips expanded, tongue ballooned, and eyelids puffed up so much it looked like my eyes had been replaced with a pair of matching arses, each with buttocks proportioned according to what would now be recognised as the Kardashian school.

In later years, my parents freely admitted they were stumped by this small-scale horror show. But rather than seek medical expertise, they went all Holmes and Watson and decided to investigate for themselves. One week they tried without the salt. Not guilty. Next week, vinegar was acquitted. Perhaps the chips?

'It was a process of elimination,' Dad would later explain, deploying the airy tone he reserved for those occasions when he wanted to impress upon me that whatever assumptions I was even thinking of making, they were wrong.

'Didn't you worry you might accidentally eliminate me?'

'No,' he said, in the same tone.

These days there are handy websites that outline the symptoms of anaphylaxis. Nestled amid its myriad horrors (facial swelling, breathing and swallowing trouble, possible death) is perhaps the greatest: 'A feeling of impending doom.'

For Mum it was a mystery as unhappy as it was unfathomable. How could food – that reliable friend, microwaveable companion, physician and nutrition all rolled into one – possibly turn foe?

She had a boyfriend who felt the same way. He was convinced (a) it all hinged on how the fish was cooked, and (b) he was the man with the know-how. Like an alchemist who specialised in Neptune's bounty, he was going to take a base material – a bream he'd hooked that morning – and turn it into the key that would unlock for me the gates to the kingdom of fish-eaters, or at the very least, navigate my gut without incident.

'Shouldn't we take him to hospital?' I heard him ask later as I twitched on the floor.

'Doctors! What do they know?' Mum replied, sounding crosser and more Hungarian than usual. 'Fark zem.'

So it was a contrast when I had my next anaphylaxis adventure, courtesy of a careless order in a Vietnamese restaurant. One of my dining companions was a trainee doctor, and she rushed me to the nearby hospital, firing medical jargon at the receptionist so rapidly I tried bending my balloon lips into a smile.

It was a Saturday night and the hospital was busy. As I lay on my bed, as festooned with tubes as the Dalek Emperor, my eyelids slowly deflated, allowing me a clearer view of my ward buddies. Given I was neither handcuffed to my bed nor assisting police with their inquiries, I was in a minority. Another positive was that I could now identify a fishcake. I told myself it wouldn't happen again. And amusingly, I believed myself.

Let's jump back to the beginning of the story, roughly 11 kilometres above the sea and much farther from any hospital or, stupidly, Epipen. In the flat, yawning hours of flight, the anticipation of the arrival of food – or at least food's closest approximation – takes on peculiar dimensions. The moment was as beautiful as I'd imagined, the trolley pulling up beside me, the beaming flight attendant standing behind it. 'Special meal for you, Mr Jeffrey!' she announced, like a lottery employee calling a winner. 'No fish!'

She handed me the box, and upon its lid was a label with my name and the magic word 'chicken'. It's possible my happiness was disproportionate, but funny things happen to human beings at high altitude. Our feet swell. Our tastebuds go awry. We dehydrate. We develop a different awareness of the passage of time. We contemplate buying duty free from a trolley.

And sometimes, we go cock-a-hoop over a lump of chicken in a box. This was surely what it was like in business class, I thought, pulling back the lid and peering through the modest wisp of steam to my fillet of white flesh upon its bed of rice. Once I'd wrestled my cutlery out of its plastic sheath, I got stuck in.

Its flavour came as a bit of a surprise, but I ploughed on. In my defence, it was airline cuisine, the least easily recognised of the food groups. Doubly so when it's chicken.

It was only after the second, queer mouthful that the terrible suspicion debuted in my mind and I turned the fillet over. At the first sight of the marks of where bones had once been – fine and unmistakably piscine – I couldn't help but giggle, a response I sometimes have when things turn completely, unmistakably and irrevocably to shit.

What were the odds of this happening? After all that careful planning, even after checking that little label, this fuster cluck of a chicken was a fish, a creature whose every appendage sounds like the French for 'the end'.

The time for giggling was short; anaphylaxis does not beat about the bush. Feeling as if I was trapped in one of those comically strange dreams – albeit one in which I was still wearing pants – I slid my tray aside. The itching in my mouth was already giving way to a sensation that felt like I'd gone bobbing for apples but accidentally swallowed a hedgehog. I knelt in the cramped loo and tried getting my fingers in my throat – a supermodel at last! But it was too late. My throat had already swollen so much nothing more was getting in, but nor was it getting out. I was as sealed as my fate was.

I stumbled back towards my seat (in an empty row, as luck had it), prickles sweeping across my skin and all the usual candidates starting to swell.

'The chicken', I panted at my flight attendant, 'was fish.'

(Years later, my big sister sent me an ad she'd torn from a magazine. It depicted a freshly cracked fortune cookie and a slip of a paper that read, 'That wasn't chicken.' She said she thought I'd find it funny.)

My findings successfully presented, I was free to embark on the worst anaphylactic episode of my life. As I sank into a weird, spasmodic darkness, I could hear my heart in my ears. I heard a lot of jittery Korean. I hurt so much I could almost see the pain in flashes of vivid, livid colour. I thought about how Nick Cave had recognised the sinister side of dinner trollies and tried to warn us in 'The Mercy Seat'.

I thought about my dog waiting for me to come home; Dad always said he had five minutes' warning of my return because the dog would hear the distant sound of my roughly tuned Celica, go bananas and race to the gate. Now and then I came to and dragged apart my Kardashian eyelids. Each time the crowd of flight attendants hovering around me, wringing their hands, seemed bigger. Later, another passenger would tell me that crew members had come from the cockpit to unhappily behold row 36.

As I drifted, I grew sure this pain – this horrid, skewering pain – would never end. I would never be able to swallow again. I would never stand on *terra firma* again. Torment and self-pity worked me over like a tag team. I would never again hear a kookaburra, nor a whip bird, and I was sad. I thought about all the kisses I would never have, which struck me as a shame, as I'd spent so much of my life not having them, and now I was and it was magnificent. I thought about never having sex again; it was only a few years since I'd discovered what all the fuss was about, and the thought that it might already be past tense made the darkness more profound. The thought that my last strudel was behind me brought a different gloom. Then I thought about not having to pay off my university student debt, and death lost some of its sting.

Of course, Death was simply window-shopping and, even though time was the only medicine on offer, I was, after several wretched hours, left safely on the shelf.

My last memory of the plane is the pilot. Korean Air was code-sharing with Ansett, and the pilot was Australian and displeased. 'A report on this will be going to Sydney,' he informed me. 'It's a bloody disgrace.'

I nodded weakly, but to be honest I was ecstatic just to be alive. I was whisked with embarrassed haste through passport control and into Seoul, where I spent my three days hobbling about, eyeing all the tasty treats my throat was too swollen to admit. But things were looking up. I had my cheap hotel room and in it, a huge bath, which I promptly filled and crawled into. I wallowed in more ways than one, but eventually pulled the plug and the water began to gush from a hole in the side of the bath and across the floor, whirlpooling briefly around a drain hole before disappearing. Whoever had bathed last had left a little surprise in the plumbing. As I watched the torrent, a used condom blasted out like a ghostly torpedo, hurtling across the tiles with unerring precision towards that drain hole.

For a brief moment, as it swirled in the sudsy vortex, it felt as if there were two of us in the room – anaphylactic and prophylactic – and then it was gone.

Eventually I finished laughing and thought, could this be God's way of assuring me I would root again? As I reached for a towel, I felt the most beautiful sense of hope and wonder growing within me. How would He let me know about the strudel?

Part 4

Heart Problems

The Ballad of the Sade* Cafe**

Frank Moorhouse

I T WAS IN the month of February, in the year 1999, while living in Cambridge as The Writer at King's College. I was inclined one night to forgo High Table and leave the gown and sherry and the scintillating conversation of the best minds of my generation behind me and to lose myself in 'town'.

I decided that I would not attend the sherry at 7.20 pm and the procession into Hall behind the President of the Table (the most senior fellow present) and, after grace, to be seated and served a beautiful meal by the butlers. And then, after dessert, to retire to the Wine Room for fruit and cheese and port and white wine. And snuff. Of course.

So, I ventured out into 'town' with a certain swagger belonging to a chap from Kings – *The Writer* from King's – choosing to wear my academic gown for the heck of it.

During my time there I had sometimes snuck off college grounds and visited the Indian restaurants and searched for decadence, without much luck. I was known, of course, at some places by now for my eccentricities regarding the making of the martini and my penchant for lone dining, cross dressing (as we know, de rigueur at King's), and sometimes for improper conduct with table attendants.

I had yet to be thrown out. True, I had been moved once or twice because of my over-friendliness to people at other tables. But on the whole, I was tolerated, even if kept under a watchful eye by the staff, and I like to think that I was well admired for my quips and sallies.

On this particular night, therefore, I was nonplussed to find my Indian restaurant declared 'full' by the maître d'. As with all rejected diners, I peered at the empty tables and suspected that I was being denied one because of some previous behaviour or because of some aberrance of appearance.

'Bookings,' the maître d' said, 'all tables booked.'

I had never had to book at this or any other restaurant in Cambridge. However, I left politely and went on to my restaurant of second choice.

Again I was told that 'all the tables are reserved'.

Outside the restaurant, in the reflection of its window, I examined my dress. I was not in a dress, I had not forgotten to put my socks on and my socks matched (this is not a sartorial requirement at King's, believe me, although there is a rule about the wearing of brown shoes and when, of which I am uncertain), or to do up my fly (ditto). That my trousers were kept up by my college tie was not out of place in Cambridge. I felt my back to check whether pinned there was a notice saying, 'Thief and Liar' or 'Child Molester' or 'Australian' placed as a 'jape' by the ever-playful students who tended to treat me, *The Writer*, as a butt for all pranks and jests and practical jokes.

At my third restaurant of choice, having met the same response, I confronted the maître d'. 'Why is it that the restaurants are booked out on this particular Tuesday?'

I did not allow a querulous tone to colour my inquiry.

'If you will observe the tables of diners already seated you will notice something,' he said, and patiently gestured at the diners.

I observed. I observed couples.

Only couples.

All with long-stemmed red roses in long-necked vases and candle-lit tables.

'I observe couples dining by candlelight,' I said inconclusively. 'I see red roses.'

'And why would that be the only clientele this particular night?' the maître d' said, leading my thinking, respectfully, in the Socratic manner.

I thought of mass marriages by Dr Moon.

I shook my head. 'Give in,' I said.

'Valentine's Day,' he said, sympathetically, breaking the news to me with a tenderness not usually characteristic of any maître d'.

'Valentine's Day?'

'Yes, Valentine's Day.'

He patted my arm. 'Perhaps a drink on the house – but I am afraid no table tonight, my dear friend,' he said in this calming voice. It reminded me of the tone of voice of the counselling that I'd had on the half dozen or so post-traumatic stress counselling situations I had experienced since being in Britain.

'Valentine's Day,' I said numbly.

'Yes.' He poured me a British 'large' drink, which never seems large to me.

'Valentine's Day is a commercial fraud,' I said. 'It was never celebrated until the last few years.'

'It started around the year 270,' the maître d' said. 'Chaucer kicked it off,' he said, pouring me a second drink. In Cambridge even the maître d' is learned. I saw couple after couple enter his restaurant with red roses, the women in little black dresses and the boys in tight jeans and pressed shirts. Very short black dresses.

'However,' he said, leaning close and whispering, 'in every city there is always one restaurant designated ...' he paused, choosing his words, 'for people such as you on Valentine's Day.'

'*Such as me?*'

'Such as you.'

'Who are *such as me?*'

'Well, single people – people without partners.'

'Or people away from their partners?' I conjectured.

He obviously did not believe that I was 'away' from my partner.

'I doubt that people *away from their partners* would wish to eat alone in public on Valentine's Day,' the maître d' said gently. 'They would be more likely to eat from the refrigerator at home. Say something eggy on toast. Waiting to take a call from their loved one perhaps ...' his voice trailed off protectively.

And, of course, although he didn't say it, the maître d' knew that Those Who Are Loved *know* when it is Valentine's Day. The others don't.

'As I say,' he said, in his now infuriatingly consoling voice, 'there are places for you to go.'

He wrote something on a piece of paper, which I took to be the name and address of a restaurant, and handed it to me.

I suggested a compromise. 'I could eat something here at the bar.'

'I don't think that would be a good idea,' he said. 'Not a good idea.'

He did not want, I could tell, a single person hanging morbidly and lasciviously around his restaurant on Valentine's Day.

He moved me towards the door.

He stood there watching as I moved down the street, which seemed now devoid of light. Perhaps he was fearful that I might return and try to gain entry to his restaurant, perhaps by alleging that I had made 'a reservation for two'. And then saying that my companion had been killed in a car accident and would not be joining me for dinner.

I went then to the address he'd given me in a dark, back lane and found the restaurant. A lane so dark and full of hopeless, sleazy promise that I was surprised I had never been in it before. The restaurant was so dilapidated and out-of-the-way that it was not pretending to be other than a Place of Last Resort for diners not welcome at Venus's table. Or Place of Last Resort for those seeking whatever.

It was where the unfit (physically and morally) and the unworthy, the unsociable, the unfortunate, the smelly, the unwashed, the profoundly demoralised, gathered to eat – and not only, I suspected, on Valentine's Day.

The place was so dim I had to feel my way and the maître d', if that was how he saw himself, with his soiled apron and collapsed chef's hat, led me to a table. All tables were tiny and designed for one person with room for a book and a small light.

Without asking, he brought me a heavy drink of some dark and fizzing alcoholic beverage that I drank without question. He did not say, 'Happy Valentine's Day' but nor did he say, 'Unhappy Valentine's Day.'

There were no flowers in sight. No long-stemmed roses. No music played.

My ears heard the sounds of the restaurant before my eyes became accustomed to the dark. Occasionally a sigh disguised as a clearing of the throat. Occasionally I heard a noise that was a cross between a cry from the soul and a cough.

There was, from time to time, audible sobbing (something I was familiar with from dining alone at Christmas).

I became aware that there were both men and women dining in this sad cafe.

No eye contact was made at any time among the diners, or the table attendants and the diners. All eyes were cast down as victims punished cruelly by the so-called Saint of Love.

I now saw the sadism of Valentine's Day.

There were no smiles and no one laughed. All read books or *The Journal of Scientific Fallacy*. Thick books, the books that people who fear running out of reading matter and being left with themselves cart around to restaurants and read on public transport.

They were all concerned to be seen as *busy readers*.

They made facial movements of agreement or disagreement with the book, some made vigorous marks in the margins or wrote copious notes in old leather-bound notebooks, or they scribbled in the fly leaf and margins or on the blank pages at the back of the book.

I opened my own big book and began to read, and to drink in that way where, without looking at glass or bottle, you reach out and refill the glass. I have no recollection of what I ate.

And then, one by one, we paid our bills and left, walking with that false steadiness and bogus purpose that the unsteady and purposeless always affect.

None of us was under the protection of any saint as we walked out into the dark.

But no. Perhaps we were watched over by other older pagan spirits (from whom the Catholic Church had stolen Valentine's Day). Those pagan spirits who visited those *such as us* now and then, on other days of our lives, if not today, and who occasionally, surprisingly, bestow upon us their own strange, aberrant, pagan gifts.

*A pun. Marquis de Sade (1740–1814) published erotic writings that gave rise to the term *sadism* – enjoyment of cruelty. Not to be confused with Helen Folasade Adu, the English-born torch singer who sings under the name Sade (pronounced by her as 'Sarday') and known among her Australian fans as 'Sadie'.

"With acknowledgment to the Carson McCullers' novella of the title *Ballad of the Sad Cafe*.

The Bride Slipped Bare

Larissa Behrendt

T HE FEAR I experienced must have been like Gloria Gaynor's in 'I Will Survive', but unlike Gloria's, my fear didn't stem from a broken heart but a broken toilet bowl.

I shall tell you more about that in a moment, but I'm here before you as a woman who's survived her fair share of harrowing, or at least profoundly uncomfortable, experiences. As an Aboriginal woman active in the life of my community, I've lived through and survived Aboriginal politics. I've worked in the legal profession for over twenty years and experienced the most profound sexism during that time, but I've survived the Law.

And I've been an academic for most of my professional life. You might think of universities as gentle environments dedicated to the exchange of ideas, but you would be so very, very wrong. Even Henry Kissinger, reflecting on his life, said the most vicious politics he ever encountered were in academia, and not because the stakes were so high but because they were so low. Try telling an academic that they're going to lose parking space privileges on campus and prepare to see a hissy fit of gigantic proportions. I've even survived fourteen consecutive days of negative stories in *The Australian*, attacking everything from my academic ability to my sex life. For a media organisation that parrots a belief in free speech, it certainly did everything it could to shut me up.

Yes, my friends, I've survived the conflict of Aboriginal politics, sexism in the workplace, passive-aggressive pettiness in academia, and the ire of Andrew Bolt and his News Corp friends. But none of that compares to the story of survival I'm going to tell you now.

I'm going to share with you how I survived my wedding night.

By way of background you have to know I spent a year working in Canada back in the 1990s, and it wasn't exactly a match made in heaven. Don't get me wrong, Canadians are lovely people and I was working with the First Nations peoples of Alberta on a treaty negotiation process, so it was work that was a great privilege to do in a culture that I found full of wisdom, compassion and generosity. But for a Triple-A Type personality like myself, they gave me some very tough love.

For example, I was told to be ready to be picked up for a meeting at 10 am at a reservation two hours north of Edmonton. It was supposed to be a day trip, so I was ready on time, neatly groomed in my suit, my killer heals and holding on to my little briefcase. The chief negotiator, who travelled in his Winnebago with his wife and three children, picked me up four hours late and with the stopping and starting, the two-hour trip took much longer than it should have. Realising that this wasn't going to be a day trip, I quickly ducked into a Walmart (luckily, they're all over the place) to buy a nightie, clean undies, toiletries and some flat shoes.

When we finally arrived at the reservation, I assumed the meeting would start straight away and I was all ready to go. Instead I was told there was to be a sweat lodge ceremony. This required the purchase of a different kind of nightie. So I had to duck back to the Walmart to buy that nightie, one that was plain and without buttons (adornments aren't allowed and the buttons are considered decorative) and some more clean undies so I could participate in the sweat lodge. Which I did, and it was wonderful and I survived, even though I thought I was going to be cooked alive.

Then it was decided that the meeting would need to take place at a different reservation. So the next morning everyone packed up and we drove in a caravan of Winnebagos, travelling north. When we arrived, I was told that the meeting would finally take place as soon as the chief returned from hunting. And that took three days.

The meeting did happen, and it was an eye-opener to be at the table. Such an insight into the things Indigenous people can achieve when they're given the chance to determine their own future, and of course it was worth it for the privilege of being able to see that happen. But I returned home a week after I was picked up from what I thought was going to be a day trip, albeit with a range of Walmart nighties and underwear.

The other thing I'll share with you is that there was a cultural protocol in the First Nations community I was living with that required you to eat whatever was given to you at a ceremony. Now moose nose, I was assured, is a great delicacy, even though my memory of it was a mixture of gristle and snot. As a guest, I always seemed to be given this very special part of the moose as a sign of respect and acceptance. So they said, and I believed them. The advice I have to pass on to you is that your best friend at a pow-wow is salt and pepper.

But I did love Canada and I made many friends, and I did feel the way of life there challenged that part of me that is rigid, with my passion for scheduling and timing. I think their tough love loosened me up.

I was challenged for a year and I survived, and then I decided it was time to go home. But like a partner with whom you have a dysfunctional relationship, Canada has always kept drawing me back, and I came to spend my honeymoon in Vancouver.

I should've known that the wedding and honeymoon were going to be complicated. My fiance, Michael, and I had originally booked a very small family wedding on Hayman Island in Queensland with a honeymoon on Beddara Island, but a storm brewed and both venues were blown away by Cyclone Yasi. Undeterred, and not taking this as a sign, we married in a small restaurant in Sydney. We had also decided to take up a work opportunity Michael had in Vancouver and add on a honeymoon. And let's face it, nothing says romance like an international financial ombudsman conference. Surely it's the next best thing to Beddara Island. Besides, we had very dear friends in Vancouver, Lea and Rick, who we wanted to see. So we felt like we were back on track after Cyclone Yasi.

Weddings, even small ones, are stressful. Ours was joyous but there was no sleep that night and we were on a plane to Vancouver the next day, and our seats were in economy so there was no sleep between Sydney and LA. We had one of those terrible stopovers that is long but not long enough to get a hotel room and sleep, so we still hadn't slept by the time we arrived in Vancouver. Lea and Rick were delighted to find they were with us – due to the time zones we'd travelled through – still on the very first night of our marriage.

They lived in a converted boat house on the First Nations reservation with a view right across the harbour back to Vancouver city. Fatigue might have overtaken us now that we'd finally arrived but for the joy of seeing these great friends. It gave us a new lease on life. We sat on their top deck enjoying the breathtaking view, sipping champagne and celebrating love and friendship.

Just as we were about to leave for dinner, Michael said, 'Look, I don't think I can go on. I'm starting to feel a little bit unsteady, like I think the whole floor's moving.'

I said, 'Sweetie, we're on a boat house, it's fine.' I encouraged him to keep going, and come to dinner with great company, great food and some great wine. Sleep could wait.

When I first contacted Rick and Lea about staying with them, they'd said, 'We've got a big place. There's plenty of room.' And indeed they did. They'd renovated their boat house beautifully and it was a three-storey masterpiece. But there was only one bedroom, up on the top floor, and they gave it to us while they took the couch on the middle floor, which they shared with their two enormous dogs.

The bedroom had an ensuite, and before I went to bed, as the real honeymoon was finally about to begin, I went to brush my teeth. There was a step down into the ensuite and … that was the last thing I remember.

I completely blacked out and I fell from the stair, hitting the edge of the bathtub with my face, right on my cheek bone. Somehow, and to this day we have no idea how I did this, I'd also broken the cistern under the toilet, causing water to gush everywhere. If there's anyone reading this now who can figure out how I physically did this, I would be most grateful to know your theories.

Anyway, Michael, hearing the loud thud, rushed to see what had happened and found me sprawled on the floor with water rushing all around me. What with rescuing me and stopping the water (which took a while to work out) Michael cut his hand on some broken porcelain. It was not serious but it bled profusely, so he was covered in blood and dripped it all over me while he picked me up and put me on the bed.

He then went downstairs to tell our hosts that we'd had this disaster and wrecked their bathroom. At one point we were worried we were going to sink their boat house, the water was gushing so forcefully. Their response? 'Yeah, we heard the noise but we knew you were on your honeymoon.' Those crazy Australians, they must have thought.

They came upstairs to survey the damage and there was water flooding the floor, a broken toilet and blood everywhere, and a semiconscious bride. We insisted on paying for the damage in this newly renovated bathroom and in true Canadian style they said, 'Oh don't even think about it, we were gonna buy a new one anyway.'

They were ready to take me to the hospital the next morning but it turned out I have a really tough head and all that was visible was a slight bruise. By lunchtime we were up in the nearby ski town of Whistler and I was nursing a cocktail.

I'd survived the first night of our marriage and our happy ever after could finally begin.

Despite the fact we trashed their house, Rick and Lea remain true friends. I did note, however, that when we were planning our last trip to meet up – going to San Francisco and the Napa Valley – I suggested to Lea that we fly into Vancouver and stay with them a while, and she said, a little too quickly, 'No, no, we'll meet you there.'

Catastrophe of Angels

Clem Bastow

IT'S A MONDAY in April, 11 am, and I am striding up Sunset en route to my first ever date in Los Angeles since moving there a month ago. Way to go, me! I think. Locking in a date before I've even signed a lease! Just wait till the folks back home hear how I've hit the ground running in Tinseltown!

Late in 2011, with $400 to my name, I decided to relocate to Los Angeles and work as a stringer – that's the English slang term for 'freelance journalists who decide to "switch things up" by relocating their life of insecure work and rental stress to sunny LA' – covering entertainment news. The subplot was that I hoped living in LA might encourage me to take my nascent screenwriting practice seriously. The thought being that if I lived in a town where one could see movies literally being made on the corner of one's street, one might be more inclined to get up at 5 am and Pomodoro Technique out a few pages.

After a month or so spent settling in, I needed material: it was time to commence dating. Nothing would make me take my screenwriting more seriously than marrying an American and getting to stay there *forever*. And it wasn't like Australia was doing much for me in that department; my last boyfriend was twenty-seven and lived in a shed. He used to encourage his dog onto the bed while we (he and I, not the dog and I) were having sex.

It's difficult to pinpoint precisely when it was I realised that the common denominator between all of my terrible dating experiences was not, in fact, that all of the guys were dickheads, but rather that the chief dickhead was me. *I am the dickhead.* Me. Because I made these choices.

'Yeah,' I'd tell friends back home, with the world-weary affectation of a global entertainment industry nomad, 'everyone does online dating here.' It's true, more people seem to rely on Match and OkCupid in that town, because unlike Melbourne, there is less of a culture of going to the pub, getting rat-arsed, then latching mollusc-like on to the first person who has more than two things in common with you. If you wake up the next day and the sight of them doesn't make you physically ill, you commence a relationship.

Here, though, I am determined to Date Distinctly American, so when 'Kraig333', who was 'looking for a Pam to my Jim' asked me out via a complicated series of photo likes and winks or kisses or g-spot massages, or whatever excruciating euphemism Match.com uses instead of 'poke', I said yes.

The date is with a forty-two-year-old writer and comic who is 5'8" – *5'8" is my absolute limit* – and seems pretty keen to meet me, if the phone conversation I had with him was any indication. *He looks good in his photo*, I think, *a bit like a young John Travolta in a good way, before the Thetans got into his weave. How bad can it be?*

The answer dawns on me when I see a small, Hobbit-like figure striding towards me. He is definitely not 5'8". He is certainly more like 5'4", in shoes. He is wearing a jacket – blazer? – made of the sort of PVC that hasn't existed since more than one in a thousand young men wanted to dress as Neo from *The Matrix*: matte and sort of spongy, like a yoga roll. I catch myself staring at it in awe when he begins to speak. His real name is Dave and he parked nearby, and why don't we drive to Veggie Grill so we have more time to talk?

I'm so bewildered by this tiny, PVC-wrapped person that before I know what I'm doing, I get into his car and am overwhelmed by the scent of cherry-flavoured Little Tree air-freshener. Is there a hint of chloroform in the base notes of this heady perfume, I think? The head-lines start to flash before me: 'Promising Melbourne writer dies abroad',

'In bitter irony, former RRR presenter Clem Bastow found stuffed in bins behind Amoeba Music', 'Complete moron gets into mysterious car with fun-sized John Travolta lookalike, pays terrible price'.

Oh no, he's reaching into the glovebox. This is it, it's all over. Here comes the gun, or the knife, or the metal dildo. My name was Clementine, and I was going to be a screenwriter. Just as I prepare myself for the sight of the weapon, he hands me a folded piece of paper.

'I printed out the menu,' he says, and it's clear he means for me to decide what I'm going to eat before we reach the restaurant (which, by the way, is definitely close enough to walk).

'Oh!' I say, with far too much relieved enthusiasm, as the car pulls away from the kerb and onto Sunset.

He puts one, two, three pieces of cinnamon gum in his mouth, tells me about how he writes the taglines for video – *not* DVD – releases. He once did one for *Melrose Place*, maybe I saw it? I tell him I wasn't allowed to watch *Melrose Place* when I was nine.

Finally, we reach Crescent Heights and pull into the Trader Joe's garage – 'Promising young writer clubbed to death with jar of Cookie Butter' – and begin the ascent to Veggie Grill. I smile at the waitress with a look in my eyes that I think says, 'Please help' but she probably just thinks it says, 'Shitty tipper.' David says my earrings, triangles of pointed plastic daubed with cheap black rhinestones, are 'making his crotch hurt'.

DaveKraig666 and I sit down at a table in the corner. He puts one, two tabs of Pepto Bismol in his mouth, leans his arms on the table like a Hill Street lawyer billboard, and says, 'So, what do you want to ask me?' I fumble and ask something about work, and he tells me he wrote a romantic comedy screenplay. Ten years ago. He's still working on it. He tells me about a short film he made that someone whose name I do not recognise thought was 'great'.

As he asks me if he'd know any of my work, and the noise in the restaurant drains away to nothing but the tinkle of ice-cubes against the iced-tea fountain's stainless-steel grille as I feel an acute sense of enlightenment: this isn't a date, I have been visited by The Ghost of Screenwriting Yet to Come!

I take his hand as he swallows some anti-anxiety medicine and we fly through space and time and smog. He shows me my 'efficiency' apartment in Koreatown in 2029. The vision is so real I can smell the mildew gathering under that one curled-up corner of parquetry in front of the small sink. I see thirty-seven-year-old me, hair greying, wearing my 'Barack to the Future' t-shirt and nothing else, working on the same fantasy adventure script I started in 2010. Behind my desk is a sole framed photograph of me at my city hall wedding to a 5'4" man in a *World of Warcraft* t-shirt.

KraigDavid69 stares at me from across the table, eating another Pepto tablet. 'Am I boring you?' he asks. I take stock of my surroundings and realise that the vision has ended. 'Hellooooo!' he says in a manner that was probably hilarious in 1996 when people still remembered lines from the heartwarming western comedy adventure *City Slickers*.

I fold my napkin and place it on the table. 'I'm really sorry,' I begin, 'But …'

He holds up a hand in protest. 'I'll be right back, I just need to visit the little boys' room.'

He shuffles off and I look around, calculating the distance to the nearest exit and wonder if I can create a distraction at the iced-tea fountain in order to make a quick get-away.

Eventually, DavidKraig returns from the bathroom and announces that the date is over, but he's going downstairs to Trader Joe's if I want to come and get anything. Bewildered, I jump at the chance to exit this West Coast reboot of *Waiting for Godot*.

For ten minutes or so, we shuffle around TJ's – as he carries a 2-gallon jug of sweet tea and a box of laundry soap, I think about the inevitability of death and whether you can truly trust anyone. Soon after, we get back into his car – 'Talented Australian screenwriter killed in six-car pile-up at Hollywood and Highland' – and talk about something I literally can't remember before I can't last another second and yell, 'I'll get out here, thanks!' We're somewhere near the end of the Walk of Fame, the bit where the names get real obscure, and nowhere near a Metro station, but even being murdered by a hotdog stand attendee on Hollywood is better than spending another second in this cherry-scented sarcophagus of sadness.

'Are you sure?' he says, leaning out the passenger window.

'Yes, totally fine!' I chirp. As I stride off, I confidently tell myself this is the last time I will ever go on a date in Los Angeles.

Six months later, it's 3 am and I am midway through what could possibly be the most excruciatingly bad sex I have ever had. As the thirty-seven-year-old aspiring actor grinds away on top of me, my mind wanders to things like, 'I wonder if my editor liked that last article', 'How many Trader Joe's coconut macaroons is too many?' and 'What did I do to deserve this?'

Hours earlier, we had agreed to meet for drinks, and so I'd performed the mating ritual of the Angeleno female: I looked at his reel on YouTube. There was a chocolate bar commercial and an excruciating improvised song about sausages, so naturally I'd put aside my better judgement and decided I would let him see me naked.

My mind drifts to the future and I think about how much I will enjoy it when he turns up to audition for a secondary role in a film I am making. 'Didn't I see you in an Almond Mounds commercial once?' I will ask from behind the camera.

Eventually the endless pummelling of my cervix becomes too ridiculous to bear and I start laughing. He doesn't reciprocate. 'You take this all pretty seriously,' I say light-heartedly.

'Yeah?' He heaves himself off me and flops down onto the bed like a fourteen-year-old throwing a tantrum. 'And you laugh too much.'

Just as things seem to be getting somewhere in the general vicinity of mutual pleasure, he rolls over me and lies back with his hands behind his head, then gestures in the direction of my laptop – my iTunes is playing – and announces, 'I'm listening to Bob now.'

We lie there for a moment, him in silent reverence in the church of Bob Dylan, me imagining shooting lasers out of my eyes at him until his skull begins to crumble before bursting into flames.

'Wow,' he says, his tone about as far from the dictionary definition of 'wow' as you can get, 'you've got a lot of deep tracks on this playlist.'

'No shit, drongo,' I feel like saying. 'I was a professional music critic for thirteen years.' But I just mumble something like, 'Oh, yeah.'

A couple of hours later, his phone alarm goes off to remind him to move his car before the parking conditions change at 6 am. 'Are you going to come back after you move the car?' I ask, in a Golden Globe–worthy impression of someone who wants someone to come back after they move their car.

'No.' He sniffs, as though I'd just asked him to meet my parents.

I consider leaping out of bed to kick the door shut after him, yelling, 'And stay out!' Instead, I roll over and start playing Bejeweled.

It is, I vow, the last time I will ever have sex in Los Angeles.

Months later, at San Diego Comic-Con, I run into a former Tinder match at a party on a pirate ship. He was a journo who, despite a few promising dates, couldn't seem to find the time in his 24/7, eight-days-a-week lifestyle for a relationship or anything resembling one.

Our little moment on the pirate ship is like something out of a rom-com: I'm busy trying to catch Henry Cavill's attention by the bar, and then I turn, the crowd parts, and I see my former match across the … floor? Deck? We're too far apart to talk, so he does an exaggerated mime that seems to imply he feels stupid for not making a go of our burgeoning relationship. I make a face that says, 'I agree, I look hot as shit.' (I do; I'm wearing elf ear tips.)

Smash cut to forty-five or so minutes later and we are making out in the concrete garden of the Gaslamp Hilton. I mention something about having soooo much stuff to bring back from San Diego to LA on the train and he says, in an incredibly hot bit of dirty talk, 'I have a car and I'm driving back solo, my friend's ended up staying longer. I can take some of your stuff back, if you like?' It's 2.45 am and I'm ready to marry a workaholic games journalist.

The next morning, he pulls up outside the Hilton and I meet him with a few boxes filled with *Game of Thrones* and *Lord of The Rings* costume ephemera, including a large swathe of swords I advise him not to keep visible while driving, you know, because of cops. We have an awkward kiss and he agrees to drop my costumes and props around at a convenient time when I get back.

I stroll back to the hotel via Starbucks, where the barista writes my name as 'Cleam', and I've never felt happier. After nearly two years in LA, things seem to be working out. I've finally met a guy who knows that the quickest way to a girl's heart is to offer to transport her 47" Anduril replica sword up the Pacific Coast Highway!

As soon as I arrive back in LA my dream of a spousal visa crumbles as I realise that my 47" Anduril replica sword is now being held hostage in the trunk of a workaholic games journalist's car. He's too busy to come over today, or tomorrow, or most of this week. Actually, how's two weeks from now for me?

Like sands through the hourglass, the next few weeks slowly stretch on until, miracle, he has a few hours in which he will be able to deliver my Comic-Con gear to my apartment.

When he eventually arrives, I'm wearing my pyjamas and eating a plate of pita breads smeared with Vegemite. He shuffles into my studio apartment, leans the swords and costume boxes against the wall, and seems to be motioning me to give him the grand tour. I oblige, taking him into the tiny kitchen where earthquakes jiggle the fridge power cord out of the wall socket, and where one day huge chunks of white plastic (and … other things) started belching out of the sink because my upstairs neighbour had used Drano after a 'big night'. I showed him the bathroom, the adjoining wall of which was thin enough that I would hear my neighbour vomiting uncontrollably at all hours.

We go back into the bedroom–living room, me holding my last Vegemite pita. He tells me he's had a bit of a cold that he hasn't been able to shake since Comic-Con. I weakly joke about 'con flu'. We both stand there for a few more minutes in silence, aside from my air-conditioner rattling in the window. Suddenly it dawns on me that he's waiting for the internationally recognised currency for transporting LARP weapons in a sporty hatchback: human sex.

Soon after that moment of realisation, we are on the bed, having sex, and all I can think about is the Vegemite pita I abandoned on the side table for this express purpose. He feels clammy and cold, and I wonder if con flu is considered a sexually transmitted disease. The sex is so bad. It's bad in a way that is ultimately crushing: almost silent, plodding, the bare minimum two human beings can give each other in the way of intimacy and a show of erotic frisson.

Seconds stretch on like hours and eventually he peels his body away from mine. The transaction complete, he gathers all his things and leaves.

After I take a shower and scrub off the con flu, I retrieve my last Vegemite pita, not yet stale, from the bedside table. I take a seat at the kitchen table, open my laptop, and eat while investigating how much it would cost to ship my entire life back to Australia, and vow never again to live in Los Angeles.

Vows, Wows and Woes

Annie Nolan

I<small>T WAS AROUND</small> the time that I found myself standing in a red-brick public toilet block, between the ceremony and photos, in a giant white gown, with my legs apart and my friends assisting me to insert a tampon, that I wondered again if this whole marriage thing was right for me.

I already had three children with Liam, our assets were tied, we already knew we loved each other, and I wasn't going to be taking his last name. Nothing was really going to change for us after marriage. And that highlights my privilege, as marriage has been used to oppress women for millennia – seen as objects going from our fathers to our husbands. Many sisters across the globe don't have a choice to enter into it like I did. I felt a pang of guilt as I felt a pang of uterine cramping.

They say that young girls often fantasise about this 'special day'. I was never that little girl. I often felt let down by the fairytales I loved because they almost always ended with the lead female character being 'saved' by an egotistical prince, and the couple kissing on their wedding day. Those princes really do have a ridiculous saviour complex, especially when the forest and ocean animals in most Disney movies did much more to help the women than they did.

But there I was, not super keen on the institution but hypocritically adorned with ring on finger and in a gown so large I was unable to navigate to my nether regions. It did have pockets though.

Where on Earth was my prince when I needed to make sure I didn't get blood on this restrictive white gown?

'Aren't you on the pill, Annie? Why the hell wouldn't you skip your period on your wedding day?' My bridesmaid laughed, holding up the dress like a blanket fort we once made as children.

'As if I planned this! After everything that's happened today, are you really surprised?' I groaned back.

I think the reason I wanted to wed all came down to my inability to control my love of parties, a dash of internalised Catholicism from a childhood raised in the Church, and my incessant need to make my family happy.

Oh, and love too. Bloody love.

Having a party was a huge factor in us picking New Year's Eve for our wedding date. However, the date proved to be an issue when it came to finding a caterer the day before the wedding, when our original caterer became unwell. As the caterer was being taken to hospital and his staff hadn't been briefed on what to do, the deliveries of fresh food were arriving. My family stepped in and took charge. I had aunties, uncles and cousins preparing food and coming up with new recipes in the kitchen. Although I really thought we should just have a barbecue and not worry about it, I was extremely grateful to my family for playing 'Ready, Steady, Cook' and putting on a feast with the random ingredients they had. On the day, the caterer was much better, so I ended up inviting him to the wedding and he helped out as a waiter. But my mother also nearly needed hospitalisation after the ordeal.

Things really didn't go to plan for Mum. She insisted that she didn't want to burden my make-up and hair people on the day so found a 'lovely lady down at the shops' to do it. A great idea, until she stormed through the door where the bridal party was getting ready asking, 'Do I look shit?'

Everyone looked at one another to see who was courageous enough to tell the truth. I don't like to criticise someone's appearance, but I could only assume that the lovely lady somehow hated my mum. Because, indeed, she looked shit. Her lips were over drawn in fluorescent pink, the woman had used heavy blue eyeliner, and Mum's eyelashes were so large they went over her eyebrows and could possibly take flight. Her hair was so tightly curled to her scalp that even Shirley Temple would say those curls needed to be brushed out.

I was the one who had to tell her.

'I knew it! I knew it. I haven't even seen myself properly yet.' She huffed despairingly as she walked up the hallway. Then seconds later, she screamed when she saw herself in the mirror. 'I look like one of those blow-up sex dolls!'

Kindly, my hair and make-up artists cast their magic and made Mum look herself again.

Moments later the flowers arrived. Flowers for another person's wedding that we didn't order. It wasn't a big deal to me, as I find it hard to get too upset about plants. My bouquet was redone with lovely roses, but yeah, I suppose it's unusual to have lots of bright gerberas as the wedding flower. Colourful though!

After that, and only minutes before the wedding, my children accidentally poured water onto the laptop from which I was going to read my vows. The bridesmaids were so stressed about it they'd wrapped a pillow around it and weren't going to tell me, hoping the laptop would miraculously dry out before the ceremony. It's hard not to look suspicious carrying a pillow to a wedding though, so I swiftly asked why they were planning to take a nap. My best friend broke the news to me.

The vows were just about the only thing I deeply cared about on the day. I was more organised about writing those promises to Liam than almost anything else at the wedding, and as I have poor eyesight I was going to read them off the laptop with zoom. I had been relatively calm up to that point, but this rattled me a little. I could feel the tears welling in my eyes and I tried ever so hard to keep looking up and suck my tongue to the roof of my mouth, so I didn't blink and let the tears shoot down my face.

By a stroke of luck, another friend had a computer and the vows were able to be retrieved from my emails. The laptop never worked again and even as I write this, I'm finding myself yelling, 'Stand back!' to my kids. I often wonder what my best friend was going to do when I found out in the middle of the ceremony that the laptop was broken.

Mere milliseconds after the laptop debacle, drivers from two different bus companies turned up to take us to the venue. (You read that right, bus companies. I told you I love partying – I couldn't stand the thought of missing out on something if I were to travel in a fancy car to the wedding instead of with my friends.) Unfortunately, there'd been a miscommunication, so we had arguing drivers out the front of the house. What happened there is a blur, but it was clearly resolved as I was ushered onto the bus and driven to the church, albeit a tad late.

Did I mention it was a record high temperature day? Over 40°C in Ballarat – a place known for always being cooler than the rest of the state.

I cringe as I write this, as these are terribly superficial issues to those facing genuine hardship. Going out to visit my younger brother's grave after the ceremony to place my bouquet on it, I was reminded that being alive but a bit stressed was, in itself, a gift.

Nevertheless, I have sympathy for the unfortunately named 'Bridezillas'. Though weddings are meant to be about two people, it's one of the rare, socially acceptable times when women are allowed to be demanding, unapologetic, in control and in the limelight. To prioritise their happiness and set expectations high.

This was the day when I'd find out whether I had an inner Bridezilla, as things continued to fall off the rails.

Especially when I saw my two-year-old twins dragging each other across the dance floor at the reception and smiling with blue mouths. There was only one thing being served with blue colouring at our wedding: daiquiris. I marched over to the kids' table and, to my horror, I saw glasses of blue drinks. Many of them nearly empty. My grandma, who had offered to care for the children, defended herself. 'Well who serves blue iced drinks that can't be enjoyed by kids on a hot day? That's just cruel.'

After a quick assessment by my relatives who work in medicine, the kids were given the all-clear to party on. But the little girls' continuous compliments – 'You look so beautiful'; 'No, youuu look so beautiful'; 'You're my best friend'; 'Well, you're myyyy best friend' – did remind me of conversations I'd overheard in the women's toilets in nightclubs.

After emergency catering, unwanted flowers, my mother's drag look, laptop failure, the chauffeurs' fight, suspected drunk kids, record-high temperatures, and an unexpected period, the wedding was drawing to a close and I was optimistic there would be nothing else that could go wrong. It was 3 am after all.

It was over. Exhausted, sweaty and cramping, I piggy-backed my inebriated new husband to our hotel. I swiped the card to get in and it buzzed back at me. I looked at the card, assuming I had done it the wrong way around, but when I tried again the lock buzzed back at me once more. We were locked out. At this point I deliriously laughed an 'Of course we are' laugh. As it turns out, the cards used to get into the hotel reset each year, and as we got married on New Year's Eve, our cards were invalid. Together we slowly walked to my parents' house, where they answered the door in a fright, as they weren't expecting us. They kindly gave up their double bed and lay on single mattresses next to us on the floor. Consummating the marriage was never going to happen on our wedding night.

I rolled into Liam's chest and couldn't stop giggling. I whispered to him, 'I bet you didn't imagine our first night together as a married couple would be in my parents' bed?'

But being together to laugh, no matter our relationship status or hurdles, meant we were fortunate. We had gone through far bigger issues than the series of events we'd faced on our wedding day – deaths, our children being born micro premature, illness. Perspective was a gift we had in our relationship. It made us love and appreciate every moment together, even when our grand plans were disrupted.

'I will love you until the moment I take my last breath, my heart beats for the final time and my brain is able to think of you no more. And if my soul is lucky enough to live on, I will search for you just to let you know one last time, that I still love you,' I said in my vows.

I look back and I can see I was right, not much did change for us. But I now know that I love being married to him. I've even come to the view that our wedding, in all its hot mess, was symbolic of the life we share together and was indeed perfect for us.

I now also know that New Year's Eve is the hardest date to get a babysitter for an anniversary.

I'll Be a Real Man

Robbie Buck

I'M BLESSED WHEN it comes to catastrophes; indeed I feel my cup runneth over, especially in my love life. Particularly in my teenage love life. So here is my catastrophic quest for love. It's my Homer-like Odyssey set in an ancient land.

This quest began in Birdsville, a small town and pub in far western Queensland, near the border with South Australia. The character in this quest is mini me, an eighteen-year-old art college student with shoulder-length hair, there with some of his art student friends to document the legendary annual Birdsville Races. But our hero has something else on his mind. Something more important than the races. He feels, no he knows, that he's in love. He's in love with a woman he hasn't seen for months and he's pining. And this woman is only about 1000 kilometres due north. Earlier on that year he'd had a very short fling with this glorious young woman from Sydney (our hero lived in Brisbane). They'd started a correspondence and began to realise that maybe they had a thing for each other.

Epic love is never easy. And it had grown harder when our young lovers were separated even further. She'd gone to live at Canobie Station, a vast cattle station up in the Gulf Country. And our hero was feeling that maybe being this close – only about 1000 kilometres away – perhaps he could go up there to see the love of his life.

You know our hero is me, so let me now reveal my love was Elizabeth. And nothing would sway me from being with her. I had an image in my head that I'd turn up at this cattle station and, a bit like a Mills and Boon novel, she would come out from the homestead and I'd be there at the gate. She would see me and she'd have the wind in her hair and she'd look out and there would be the love of her life. We'd have our arms out and we'd run towards each other and embrace. This vision made me brave.

Most people fly into Birdsville, so I thought it would be easy to get a lift in a plane to Mount Isa. From there I could hitch to see my girl. So on the final night of the Birdsville Races, after a few schooners, I went around to everybody in the pub and said, 'Are you leaving tomorrow in a plane and are you going to Mount Isa and what are the chances of getting a lift with you?'

Now what was amazing about this was that I was offered a lift to Adelaide, a lift to Brisbane, a lift to Perth; I was offered a lift to pretty much every part of the country, but I wasn't offered a lift to Mount Isa. Until finally the last fellow I spoke to said, 'Look, I'm going to Mount Isa tomorrow, but I'm not flying. I'm driving.' I didn't even know there was a road to Mount Isa but he assured me there was, and while it was only open about three months of the year, it was open at the moment. My noble new friend slurred, 'It's going to take me two days, but if you are serious, meet me at my tent at 6 am tomorrow and if you are there you get a lift.'

Beauty.

I turned up in the morning and he seemed a bit surprised to see me as he'd had more than a couple of drinks the night before, but he was a man of his slurred words. It did occur to me at this stage that I was only eighteen and I've never met this guy before and we were going off to the desert together for two days. But I knew that Elizabeth loved me as much as I loved her, and she was really going to appreciate the fact that I was doing this for her. So off we went. And it was actually a really beautiful couple of days. The guy was a builder from Melbourne and he was pretty generous. We had to stay at a little homestead halfway along the track. He paid for that, he bought me dinner, he bought me a drink, and he was very honourable. He said to me over dinner, 'We'll be in Mount Isa tomorrow. Are you going to be all right?'

I said, 'Yeah, no worries, I've got this all worked out. It's Monday and I know there's a mail van that goes from Julia Creek up the road past Canobie Station. It leaves at four o'clock every Wednesday morning. So I've got plenty of time to get to Mount Isa, hitch to Julia Creek, find the mail man and then convince him to give me a lift.' My friend lifted his eyebrows but did not sway me from my quest.

The next day, my honourable mate dropped me off on the outskirts of Mount Isa. As I stood beside the road, my thumb outstretched, I was feeling pretty proud of myself. I thought, This is what real men do. I am becoming a real man and I am doing what real men do. I'm going off to see my real woman and together we are going to be perfect. We are going to be people. We may even make people.

I must say I felt a little less manly after a few hours as cars drove past and no one picked me up. Finally, a white panel van stopped. In the world of hitching, panel vans are always a bit dodgy. But there was only one guy in it so I thought it should be okay. I got in and met Colin, who asked, 'Where you heading?' Turns out he was heading to Julia Creek too. He told me it was about 250 k and we'd be there in a couple of hours.

Off we drove into the desert. It was hot and we saw the occasional mirage that looked like water, but there was not much else to see and we didn't have much to say. Let's face it, we were a tough-looking bloke in a panel van and an eighteen-year-old, long-haired art student. The nexus was not that deep. Then, out of this vast mirage and milky haze, we saw an apparition up ahead – a little red dot. We kept driving and Colin said, 'There's something up there.' Then he floored it so fast that we soon realised we were catching up with the back of another panel van. Colin said, 'Shit, that looks like Jacko's van.' And I thought, one panel van okay, two not great.

We came alongside the other van and a face turned and looked at me, and this face had lots of jail tattoos and big straggly hair and there was another face equally menacing right next to him. And I thought, really not great, but kind of exciting. The boys were certainly very excited to see us. 'Pull over, pull over,' they yelled. We pulled over. Now at this stage of my quest I was still holding that vision of Elizabeth at the front of the homestead, and as we pulled over in a cloud of red dust I began to think what a great tale this will be to tell her. I imagined her realising just how much of a quest I had come on to see her, and how much dedication I had to the relationship. I hadn't actually rung Elizabeth prior to this because these were the days before mobile phones, we didn't even have email; we actually sent letters to each other. I was lost in a momentary reverie of how much she would be surprised and thrilled.

But as we pulled over to the side of the road I realised that we were about 80 kilometres from Julia Creek, and I was mindful that I had to be there that night as the mail van would be leaving before dawn. The timing was critical. We leaned out of the car to chat, and the tattooed blokes in the front seat said, 'Colin, mate, haven't seen you in ages. How you going and where you going?'

Col answered, 'We're going to Julia Creek.'

And I said, 'Yes, yes we are and it's going to be great.'

Then they said, 'No, mate, we're going to camp up here on the creek bed. You should camp with us.'

My heart sank and I said pathetically to Colin, 'Please no.'

But Colin looked at me and looked at his mates, and he said, 'Yeah, bloody good idea. Let's do it.'

We pulled off the road onto a dry creek bed and drove a couple of kilometres to a little spot in the middle of the desert, and my quest seemed thwarted. But real men do not give up in the face of failure, so I told my new mates I was going to try to get a lift, and I walked back down to the road.

By now it was getting towards dusk. Big trucks came past but hardly any cars. No one stopped for me. Two hours later I realised it was nearly dark and I was done. I went back to the campsite, noting that they'd pulled out the Jim Beam and were getting a bit rowdy. Now it's fair to say they were less than enthused to see the return of the long-haired art college student. I tried to ingratiate myself with these young men but what I hadn't realised when we first pulled off was that there were another three in the back of the panel van, and they were all having a lovely conversation about the revolver they'd buried so the police couldn't find it, and about their sawn-off shotgun.

I was not excited about this. I was even less excited when they pulled the sawn-off shotgun out of the back of the van. They were wondering if I'd like to have a go of it, but I said, no, I didn't think so, but thank you very much. But they insisted.

I can now say I've fired a sawn-off shotgun. And as fun as that was, I soon decided it would be better if I were to retreat and go to sleep. I said, 'Guys, thanks for such a fun night. I won't forget this in a hurry. I'm going to roll out my sleeping bag and have a kip.' I knew I'd missed the mail van, but I had bigger things to worry about because they were still drinking.

I walked about 30 metres and found a spot to lie down, and I pretended to go to sleep. I obviously couldn't sleep because I was completely freaking out. This was when things got a little dark.

While I was lying there on edge, wide awake, listening to them, one of them asked Colin, 'So ah, who's the little fucker?' and Colin answered, 'I don't know, mate. I picked him up in Mount Isa. It was a mistake.'

For a moment I was hurt. I thought, that's a bit cruel, I thought we were getting on all right. And then one of them said, 'You know what we should do? We should smear a bit of Vegemite on his face, that would give him a shock, wouldn't it.'

Then the other one said, 'No, no, we should give him a bit of a kicking. See what that does for him.'

Then there was a lull in the conversation before the particularly nasty one said, 'We should string the little cunt up in the fucking tree.'

It was at this point I thought, gee, I'm really in trouble.

But I was no art student wuss. I was tough. This is how tough I was – I had a Swiss Army knife. So, heart pounding and skin sweating, I very quietly reached into my bag and pulled out my Swiss Army knife and opened the blade. I thought, well, there's five of them, they've got a sawn-off shotgun and I've got my Swiss Army knife. And just at that moment, for the first time, I thought maybe it wasn't worth seeing Elizabeth.

I truly believe there was a critical moment when it could have gone either way. People have asked me since if the men were playing with me and just trying to intimidate me. But no, I knew it was real. I knew that if the mood had not switched, they could have gone, 'Let's do this.'

And they would have and they could have. Luckily the tension cracked just for a moment and they went off in a different direction in their conversation. Then, one by one, thanks to Jim Beam, they passed out around the fire; it was like watching flowers close. When the last one fell, I started to breathe again. Then, knife still ready, I waited half an hour. After that I got up, packed my stuff, and tiptoed out of the campsite and walked down to the highway.

I waited there for hours as trucks came past. No one picked me up. But just before dawn, when I was growing desperate and terrified the blokes would wake up and come and find me, I saw a vision. Out of the dawn light a four-wheel drive snaked across the horizon. It was so beautiful – the outback red, the blue light of the sky and this green LandCruiser. I stood in the middle of the road and put my hand out. I thought, you can run over me, mate, but I'm not getting out of your way.

The bushy pulled up and he said, 'What the hell are you doing here?'

'Let me in and I'll tell you everything,' I said. 'Please just drive.'

As we took off in a plume of dust, I told him what happened. He said sweetly, 'You, my son, are an idiot. You would not believe what goes down on this road. But calm down, I've got double tanks, I can outrun anyone.'

Thanks to my blessed saviour, I got to Julia Creek. I was alive. I was not strung up. But I'd missed the mail van.

Now my quest was even more desperate. I had to make this hell worth it by wrapping Elizabeth in my battle-scarred arms. I harassed the customers at the local service station, asking each and every one with wheels if they were going past Canobie Station. Five hours later a bloke offered me a lift. And despite all my stuff-ups I'd still not learned anything about planning. Again, I jumped in a car without forethought or many provisions. My reasoning was that I deserved my date with my girl, and the horror was over. I figured that the homestead couldn't be far from the road as it was built in 1856 when they used horses, so I should be able to walk from the road to my gal.

I got dropped at the front gate of Canobie Station with a light heart, 2 litres of water and a can of fruit. Off I trekked along the road to my sweet woman.

It was 35 degrees and I walked for three or four hours. Nothing. Eventually I found a turned-over semi-trailer and I climbed up, thinking I'd see the homestead or the windmill. I couldn't see a thing. Nothing. I walked all the way back to the front gate and I sat down, feeling hot, thirsty and terrified. I'd finished my water and I had just opened fruit salad when a four-wheel drive came along. The guy wound down his window and said, 'What the hell are you doing?'

'I'm here to go to the homestead. Can you give me a lift?'

He said, 'Look, mate, I come here once a month, and maybe once a week someone comes out of the homestead onto this road. You would be dead in a day in this heat without water.'

I have to admit I was chastened by this near-death experience. But as we drove to the homestead, which was about 20 kilometres down unmarked tracks, I was thinking, Well, it's been hell. I've nearly died. Twice. But it'll be worth it. Because sometimes you've got to sacrifice things for love.

After all the horror, the image of Elizabeth in the homestead came back into my head, and I felt a sense of delight that I'd made it. Homer was returning. The Odyssey was over.

But Elizabeth did not run out of the homestead, wind in her hair and arms outstretched. I found her out the back of one of the sheds, and she did not look surprised and thrilled. She looked shocked and grumpy. She immediately informed me she was seeing Gary, the chief jackaroo.

And that was my catastrophic quest for love …

How to Lose Your Mind in Ten Dates

Estelle Tang

I T IS ALMOST too unbearably Carrie Bradshaw to explain how I ended up holding a human-sized, tiger-print leather collar in a stranger's apartment, deciding whether I should do what he had asked and put it around his neck. It sounds cribbed from *Sex and the City*, like I purposely moved to New York to gin up juicy material for my memoirs, of the kind that will definitely upset my parents.

But trust me: I did not move halfway around the world to generate self-deprecating jokes about my romantic idiocy or to rack up inheritance-voiding antics. Unlike that perfect noughties love sprite Carrie, I have never spent $1000 on a pair of shoes. I have never, thank goodness, been dumped on a Post-It. Neither have I met a Mr Big, or even a Mr Kind of on the Bigger Side. But there's a reason *SATC* is set in this magnificent nightmare of a town. Dating in New York City is like competitive eating: not for beginners, and it can make you sick.

When I broke up with my boyfriend of fourteen years a couple of years ago, I was thinking, shit, I'll have to move. I was thinking, I don't know how to be alone. I was thinking, I won't be able to split Ubers anymore. I was not, however, on top of the fact that I'd spent the whole of my adult life in a relationship and had, therefore, never learned how to date. So, eighteen months later, when the dust had settled and I was feeling ready to meet people, I was at a loss. Like ice skating or speaking Russian or making pierogi from scratch, it was an activity I had zero experience with. But even more than those pursuits, romance was uniquely befuddling. It was a realm of no correct answers, endless permutations, and the persistent threat of embarrassment. Help, I thought.

The few relationships I'd been in had begun in more traditional ways: not running away when someone who was throwing up after a few too many cans (an extremely romantic gesture when you're eighteen and have known each other for about thirty-seven minutes), or going over to someone's house to 'watch *Finding Nemo*' (a terrific movie). In these scenarios, all I'd had to do was basically be there. Easy! In Australia, when you're young, you pash under the plausible deniability aegis of alcohol; when you wake up the next morning, if you're both still into it, you're basically hitched.

In contrast, New York, the conveyor belt of underwhelming pop culture liaisons, a city continually replenished with coltish twenty-three-year-olds who are richer than you, and anecdotally known as the worst place in the world to seek *l'amour*, felt a little more intimidating. Anxieties about how to approach dating – Who did I want to date? How would I find these people? How many axe murderers are still around in this day and age, do you think? – came at me like a fusillade from one of those tennis-ball machines. It was all too much. Still, I knew I had to get there somehow. The only thing to do was tackle it like any other problem: systematically. Courtship was alien to me, so I'd have to work it out bit by bit.

I pondered my approach. First of all, I'd have to actually, well, date. I complained to my friends. 'I don't know how to *do* this. I'm a grown woman and I feel like a baby. Will I have to use an app? I'm so stressed.' I must have annoyed people enough to inspire them to help me, because one evening, on the way to meet a friend, she texted: *I'm with a guy I know. He's cute and single. Do you want me to bring him?*

My eyes widened like a manga character's. As with my early love experiences, all I would have to do was *be there*. Was forcing other people to do the work the secret to romantic success? The lazy oaf in me rejoiced. *Sure whatever LOL*, I typed, poetically. And after we all had a couple of wines together, I did actually exchange numbers with him. Weeks later, we hung out, and while it wasn't earth-shattering, it was totally, completely, 100 per cent okay.

I was thrilled. Could it really be that straightforward? Quickly, though, I came to my senses. The universe wasn't going to just throw eligible people in my lap like that forever. I didn't like the idea that I wasn't in charge of my fate; I needed to be at the steering wheel at least somewhat. What if I asked all my friends to set me up? A genius solution. I was going to conquer this weird little dilemma.

Nevertheless, I was about to learn that plenty of elements could still defy my control – and that there's no way to be good at dating without making approximately one billion mistakes first.

You might think that dating is one skill, but in actual fact, it comprises many, many smaller skills. Not only do you have to find someone you want to spend one to three hours with in the near future, but you also have to know how to find a bar that's not so busy you can't find a seat, though not so quiet you'll feel like everyone's listening to you. You have to know how to talk about yourself without making someone fall asleep; you have to know how to tell the same stories over and over again without falling asleep yourself. You have to be able to end a fizzling conversation politely and exit a dead-end situation gracefully. And I was about to find out that I didn't know how to do any of this.

My friends did their jobs beautifully, and hand-selected five very nice people for me. But even with that advantage, it was still a rather Sisyphean endeavour. I hate the idea that finding someone to be with is a numbers game. But dipping my toe into the man pool proved that the human lottery's odds are just as bad as a scratchie's.

Date #1 … well, we'll come back to him. Date #2 was a lovely guy who informed me cheerily that our visit to the cinema was the first time in his adult life he'd seen a movie not stoned, which I wasn't morally opposed to at all, but I personally had never been high, and we called it quits after a couple of hangs. Having been divorced over a year ago, Date #3 treated me to two extremely nice dinners before deciding to reconcile with his ex-wife. (I'm always happy to be a stepping stone towards destiny.) Date #4 lived upstate and was rarely in the city, so seeing him was logistically trying, and date #5 was a delightful big WASPy man who was also already seeing about seven other people. I don't like group activities, so that was the end of that.

But back to #1. I arranged to meet him – let's call him Henry – at a bar near his apartment. He seemed perfectly nice, a little on the quieter side. Having told Henry that I was new to dating, I allowed myself some nosy questions about his romantic past. 'I haven't been in a relationship for a while,' he told me, 'but I've been dating around. Actually, a friend of mine told me she couldn't invite me to parties anymore, because I've basically hooked up with all her friends.'

I knew I was going to marry him right then. Just kidding! Still, as soon as he said that, I relaxed; he was honest, I couldn't really feel a spark between us, and I had the licence to talk to him about whatever I wanted. Perfect: a real live someone I could shamelessly siphon romantic wisdom from.

Unfortunately for him, that meant it was question time. After ordering a second glass of wine, I peppered him with borderline-rude personal inquiries (which I'm told people find extremely sexually appealing). What did he do on dates? How did he meet people? How many relationships had he been in? Obligingly, he answered my queries. Then, of course, he had some of his own. When my barrage of spiky questions finally slowed, he turned to me and said, 'Have you ever been to Burning Man?'

For those not familiar, Burning Man is a temporary terrordome conjured from dust, glitter and giant sculptures made of tetanus and rich people's dreams. Or, more simply put, it's a weeklong communal event that makes Woodstock sound like your niece's first speech night. Hardy souls head out to the Nevada desert to find themselves (and drugs and people to have group sex with); it doesn't have fans, but rather, devotees. This should be good, I thought. I told him I'd never been. 'I've gone a few times, actually,' he said, more animatedly than he'd relayed anything else all night. I became alarmed; going to Burning Man once could be the result of natural curiosity. Returning year after year? That's something like religion.

Another question swiftly followed. 'Is that a tiger?' he asked, gesturing at my left hand. I looked down at the silver ring I was wearing.

'No, it's a bear,' I said.

That was no matter. 'I love tigers,' he said, with increasing vim. 'The people I go to Burning Man with all love them. When we get there, we just ... *are* tigers.'

My face immediately went to 'nonplussed', and there was nothing I could do to hide it. It's possible he didn't notice, because he was suddenly scrolling through his Instagram to show me photos. A grid of images populated the screen, featuring dust-doused people festooned in black and orange, arranged aboard something that resembled a marooned pirate ship. It looked like a promotional poster for *Cats*. 'Oh,' I said.

My glass of wine was empty. I did not think this man was going to be my boyfriend. But when he said, 'Do you want to get something to eat?' all I could think was: How can a person ... be a tiger?

'Sounds great!' I chirped. I was learning so much.

At an izakaya-style bar, we started on a bottle of sake and picked at snacks. I was ready. *Too* ready. 'So, do you ... prowl around on all fours?' I asked.

'Not everyone,' he said, forking fried chicken onto his plate. 'We do wear a lot of tiger-print clothing.'

The world is so wide, I thought, like a wonder-filled Fraulein Maria of sexual anthropology. I was obsessed with these big cat fiends, and there was another question I wanted very badly to ask. There was no easy way to put it, so I just went the blunt path. 'Is the tiger thing ... a sex thing?'

Henry's eyes flicked to my face. 'There's something I want to show you. Want to come back to my apartment?'

Which is how I found myself in his very beautiful Manhattan studio. It had exposed brick walls and enough space to fit a couple of grand pianos. Henry offered me a drink, some obscure brownish spirit I'd never heard of, and I perched on the edge of the couch, cautiously exhilarated. I was doing great, or, at least, fine. He disappeared into a walk-in closet and emerged with a wooden chest. As he pulled various tiger-print garments out of it one by one – leggings, a mesh top, some drapey, cape-ish thing – I started to feel flutters of panic in my chest. Someone who owns a custom-made leather jacket with animal-striped trim is not kidding around.

Let me be clear: I wasn't judging him. Each to their own; I'm not fussed. But while I couldn't get enough of his tigerish lifestyle stories, my intellectual interest was not matched by any kind of romantic interest. Having made it this far, I wasn't sure exactly how to leave or backtrack. My brain activity, stymied by liquor, fumbled for a next move.

Before I could decide on anything, Henry halted the fashion show, and looked at me intently. 'There's one more thing. But it's not in the box,' he said. Curiosity killed the cat, but there was no way this guy would harm any feline.

'I'd love to see it,' I said. Back he stalked to the wardrobe. When he returned, he was in possession of a metal leash that ended in a tiger-print leather collar. It hung off his fingers, glinting.

'What do you do with this?' I asked carefully.

'Usually, I'll put it on women,' he said. 'But what I'd really like' – a brief pause – 'is to have someone put it on me.'

One thing I learned about myself that night was that, when faced with an unusual proposition I'd have little interest in, I'm apparently able to visualise and seriously consider it, even (or perhaps specifically) after five drinks. Could I assist this nice man? I didn't think I'd even have to take my clothes off. Had I, with my assiduous study of dating, been unwittingly preparing for a hyper-specific, next-level challenge of this kind?

Part of me thought I could take it on, channel my inner Carrie and take this kitty for a walk, just to see what it would be like. But part of me was tired, and as well versed in human–tiger lore as I could ever hope to be. By this time, though, I felt pretty fond of Henry and I didn't want to punish his vulnerability with a rebuff.

I wasn't going to be able to give him what he wanted. But I thought I knew how to conclude the evening to our mutual satisfaction. 'Do you like being told what to do?' I asked. He nodded. 'Henry, this has been very nice. You're going to kiss me, and then I'm going to go home,' I said, an edge of command in my voice.

'I understand,' he said, seeming pleased to have some direction. He leaned in and kissed me softly.

'That's good,' I said. And it was. I thought we both did pretty well, in the end.

Part 5

Completely Catastrophic

Flat Packed Fuck Up

Rebecca Huntley

MY FULL CATASTROPHE is all about the time I went to IKEA four times in eleven hours.

Let me be clear, I wouldn't normally have anything bad to say about a Scandinavian institution. They tend to do extremely well – you've got your Finnish schools, your Danish design, your Swedish pornography. In fact, I've had a long and lustrous relationship with IKEA.

My first job out of high school was working in the cafe of what was then the only IKEA in Australia, at the Super Centa in Moore Park. The key to the success of Cafe IKEA was that it served no Swedish food whatsoever. It was the 1990s, so I made toasted focaccias filled with roasted capsicum, ham and cheese for the overly entitled eastern suburb families that would flock there daily. These were pre-babychino days, at the apex of public interest in banana smoothies. Well-coiffed mothers would order a coffee for themselves and a banana smoothie and a blueberry muffin for their kid. I don't know what kind of explosive device they put in those freaking muffins, but as soon as they hit the Laminex tables they would burst into a million pieces, taking the smoothie down with them. And all of those crumbs and the banana goo would combine and create a thick paste. I'd have to get down on the floor and use genuine force to remove it. Despite those hazards, it was a fun job and there was a terrific camaraderie amongst the staff. I think that's because we all knew we were destined to leave Cafe IKEA in the future and buy over-priced homes that we could only afford to fill with IKEA furniture.

Fifteen years later, after my time at Cafe IKEA, I was married and we were living in the eastern suburbs and our home was full of IKEA furniture. We had couches, we had ottomans, armchairs, coffee tables, everything, all bought and constructed without an ounce of domestic strife. I mean I didn't call my husband a cunt once in any of the trips to buy the furniture or to build it.

I soon became pregnant with a little muffin–smoothie destroyer of my own. My sister in-law had given birth to her first child a few months before and they'd call her Scarlett India. I asked her, 'Where does the India come from?' and she said, 'Oh, it's where she was conceived.' So for many months we called our unborn cherub Norsberg. Although that's kind of more of a boy's name.

I should have realised that my positive relationship with IKEA couldn't last.

A few years ago, the executive team of IKEA in Australia approached me to see if I'd address their annual offsite conference. They wanted me to provide a one-hour presentation on current and future consumer trends and how they might impact on IKEA's business. In my day job I'm a social researcher, which means I conduct focus groups and surveys that provide insights to clients to help them with their business. Insights like Australians love horses but not in their meatballs. I said I'd love to come and talk to their team, and this is my usual fee for a customised, one-hour presentation to a massively successful, hugely rich, multinational corporation. The answer came back, 'Oh, I didn't realise there'd be a fee involved.' So I was like, here's an option, why don't I prepare my talk, break it down into 27 different parts, send it to you with wordless instructions on how to put it back together, and you can deliver it your fucking self?

This all brings me to the time I went to IKEA four times in eleven hours with two-year-old twins.

What made my husband Daniel and me decide to do this? Well, the twins were starting to climb the sides of their IKEA cots in an endearing attempt to kill themselves as a way of getting back at their parents for insisting they go to bed before 1 am. Over the Christmas break – yes, the Christmas break – we thought, look we'll buy them new beds.

We drove to IKEA in Tempe, bright and early so we could arrive as soon as the doors opened. But, on the way the twins fell asleep, so Daniel circled the parking lot over and over while I went in to find the beds we wanted, made a note of the different pieces we needed, and then dragged the boxes off the shelves and loaded them onto steel trolleys. One of the pieces I was looking for was a slatted bed base called the Luröy, so I grabbed two and picked up a $1 soft-serve cone on the way out. Licked it, dropped it on my foot, cleaned it up. Then I exited the building, left the boxes near the lift, and chased my husband around the IKEA parking lot until he saw me. We strapped everything onto the roof of the car and started to drive home. Then it started to rain, not heavily, but enough that when we got home, we had to tear the sodden cardboard from the boxes before we brought them into the house. The twins were awake now and hungry. I think they could smell the scent of forsaken soft-serve on my feet, and they were screaming.

As I fed them, my husband started to assemble the beds, and we quickly realised we had the wrong Luröys. They were too small. Shit. I'd already dismantled the cots at five o'clock that morning and we'd promised a friend we'd give them one of the cots the next day. So we fed the kids, changed them, then got back in the car to return the two Luröys and pick up the new ones.

On the way the girls started to lose it. Understandably, they didn't want to go back to IKEA, and they started to scream. So we made a detour to my mother's place, halfway between IKEA and our house. As we unloaded the girls, we made a plan – Daniel would return the undersized Luröys and get the new ones. We had a scheduling issue though. We had to pick up our eldest daughter from the airport as she was arriving home from holiday with her uncle and aunt. So, off Daniel went while the twins and I watched cartoons at my mum's place. Time passed. Daniel returned with our eldest daughter, her aunt and uncle, without the smaller Luröys, but also without the larger ones. 'What happened?' I asked, not calmly.

Apparently there had been a long line of frustrated people at IKEA's return counter, all crying, pulling their hair, the works, which meant it had taken him a long time to return the Luröys and left him no time to get the new ones before he had to head to the airport. So, we decided to leave all the children at my mother's house and return to IKEA on our own. The traffic was terrible, but at last we arrived. I told my husband he should go in and find the right Luröys as I seemed incapable of performing this simple task. He went in, he came out, he had the right Luröys. But also a hot dog, two packets of frozen waffles and two boxes of those alphabet biscuits. I ate an entire box of biscuits in seven minutes.

We picked up the kids, went back to our place, unloaded the car, then we put the Luröys together.

They were the wrong Luröys; they were too small – again. And then it dawned on me. Luröy is Swedish for 'sucker'. There are lots of Luröys and they are different sizes, but most of all, they are just a way for those Swedish bastards to sell hot dogs. Anyway, we decided to put everyone back in the car. Daniel didn't trust me. He said, 'You didn't pick the right Luröys.'

'Neither did you. We're all going.'

'I don't trust you, you don't trust me. Yes, we're all going.'

Agreed. We loaded everyone into the car. It was getting late, it was getting dark, our eldest child had a heat rash that was just about all over her body. The twins were screaming so loudly I thought their jaws were going to dislocate. And the traffic was terrible. We arrived, everyone got out. Like the best Swedish pornography, I thought, let's just go in the back door. We gave everyone a soft-serve cone to shut them up. Sofia was starving, we hadn't fed her at all; we'd forgotten. She ate it, and told me she felt sick. The twins just kind of put it in their hair as they do all the time with their food. We rushed around to find the elusive Luröys. We measured them to make sure they were the right ones – this was something, perhaps, we should have done previously. We miraculously found an IKEA staff member hiding behind a display gazebo and we asked her, 'Are these the right Luröys?' At that moment I would have gladly presented five hours of social trends to the IKEA management for free, just for a statutory declaration to say that these were the right Luröys. We got everyone back into the car. They were sticky, they were sickly, they were angry. We drove home. We kept the children strapped in the car, we rushed into the room. Everyone was screaming.

They fitted.

I Love Dick

Ivan Coyote

O N 19 APRIL 2016, I was walking from my apartment to the market along a very busy street in East Vancouver. About a half a block up I saw something that just seemed a little off to me somehow. Maybe it was a body language thing; maybe it was my heightened trans person's spidey senses when it comes to anticipating violence or potential danger, but I saw an interaction that seemed wrong, and I wasn't wrong. As I got closer I could hear what he was saying.

A very large man was looming over a young woman who was sitting on a bus stop bench, and he was screaming right into her face. She was young, maybe nineteen or twenty, and exceptionally beautiful. She was wearing a sleeveless, floral-patterned dress. She had headphones in her ears and appeared to be trying to read a book. The man must have weighed about 280 pounds [130 kilograms] and was in his late forties.

He was so angry his white face was red like a tomato and he was spraying spit everywhere. 'What the fuck is wrong with you?' he was saying. 'Why can't you even say hello to me, Bitch? You're a stuck-up little bitch.'

She was visibly scared, shaking and silent. I was about to intervene when I was intercepted by a tiny, fierce-looking woman in her early eighties, I would say. She squared off and gave the man a solid tongue lashing in a heavy South American accent, finger shaking and saying he was twice the young woman's age and twice her size. Did his mother know he roamed the streets talking to girls like this?

He sneered and called her a dried-up old cunt. That's when I swallowed and stepped up, saying, no, no, he couldn't speak to anyone like that.

'Stay out of this, faggot,' he said, and pulled his ham-shaped fist back, but then the bus pulled up and he turned and got on it. The young woman did not. She watched the bus pull back into the traffic, and then turned back to the old woman and me, and burst into tears.

'Oh, my god, thank you both so much. I knew it. I should have just worn a flour sack or something, but I had a job interview. I just wanted to look nice, you know, I want this job so bad. I need to get out of my parents' place and move into the city. That was the third time it's happened to me today, and you were the only ones who said anything. One dude followed me right off the train, all the way down the block. I was so afraid, and nobody helped me until now. Next time I will wear a flour sack to take the bus and get changed when I get there.'

We all exchanged names and hugs. We told Alicia from the suburbs that she should be able to wear whatever she wanted and take the bus unmolested. Maria from Costa Rica told me I was a nice gentleman, and I did not correct her.

When I got home I wrote a quick little post on my public Facebook author page, something to the effect of:

Dear dudes, yes, all men: she's wearing headphones AND reading a book. This is code for she is not interested. She knows she looks beautiful. She is not obligated to smile at you. If she's being polite to you it might be because she knows that if she isn't you might get nasty, even violent, and this is a lesson she was taught as a very little girl. She's not wearing that dress for you. She's not on the bus to meet men, it's public transit. Leave her alone. Tell your friends.

I hit *post* and forgot about it.

Until about an hour later when I picked up my phone and it said I had 2000 notifications. Within a couple of hours my post had gone viral, and over the next few days it was reposted or written about on Boing Boing and Reddit and HuffPost, and translated into Spanish and Portuguese and French and Czechoslovakian and Russian. Media contacted me for quotes. I was invited by a Russian feminist discussion group to Skype into one of their meetings. They really wanted to speak to a feminist man, they wrote me.

I said sure, but I didn't identify as a man. I was a non-binary trans person, I told them.

'Oh,' they replied. 'Then we are not interested.'

That short, unedited, nearly punctuationless post of mine has now been viewed more than any other string of words I have ever written in any of my twelve books and two decades of writing and publishing. In retrospect, I really wish I had considered paragraphs or line breaks, but who knew?

In the midst of all of this came the abuse. The MRA (Men's Rights Activists) army was deployed. Thousands and thousands of comments and emails and tweets from men who took issue with anyone saying that they did not have the right to the time and attention of any woman in public, any time, anywhere. Most of them assumed I was a man, and a man saying these things to other men sent them into a kind of collective fury and rage. Vitriol. Threats of violence. Dick pics. Disgusting screen caps of women's faces with ejaculate all over them. Jokes about the size of my penis. I had to look up the words 'chode' and 'cuck' and 'neckbeard' and 'white knight'. My favourite insult was 'Dickless wonder'. I think that would make a great t-shirt slogan, right? *Dickless Wonder, that's me.* I like it.

I got death threats. Slurs, levelled not just at me, but also at the many, many women and girls who were commenting on my page as well.

But in the midst of the misogyny and entitlement and abuse there emerged a vital conversation. Women telling their own stories about unsolicited attention. On buses and streets, at work, in parks, on aeroplanes and trains – everywhere. It had started when they were ten or eleven years old, some women said. It happens every day, they said. A real and powerful and painful conversation grew by the minute. I was moved and awed and honoured to host it.

I became a kind of accidental moderator. I deleted any comment that included the words 'pussy', 'bitch', 'cunt', 'faggot' or 'feminazi'. I erased anything that included a rape threat or was overtly rude. Hundreds and hundreds a day. I got a repetitive strain injury that still ails me to this day (they call it Millennial Thumb) from swiping and hitting *ban delete* so many times on my iPhone. I wanted the conversation to be kept safe enough for women to come and share their stories.

Every morning upon waking I would delete nasty comments for a couple of hours, and then several times during the day. The misogynists were especially active in the EU and Australia during the Canadian night.

One morning I awoke to an email that read *I Love Dick* in the subject line. I sighed and swiped left to delete it, but luckily something else caught my eye: new Amazon television series by producer of *Transparent*, Jill Solloway.

Apparently, she had seen me on YouTube or somewhere, and she wanted me to come and audition to play the part of a – get this – butch writer living in an Airstream trailer. *Play?* I thought. I was perfect for this role. I would be playing Kevin Bacon's love rival. Story of my life, I thought.

I enlisted the help of an actor friend and she coached me for my big audition. But I never heard back, so I can only assume at this point that I did not get the part.

A couple of days ago my original post was picked up again by a huge online feminist news site, and the slew of abusive comments and name calling has begun anew. So I know my shot at the Hollywood big time is coming around again soon. Any time now I will get the audition call.

Orange is the New Black and *The Handmaid's Tale*, I await your correspondence.

And this time, I am ready.

Stung

Santilla Chiapinge

ROM AS FAR back as I can remember, I've never liked maths. I had some great maths teachers during my school years, but even their support wasn't enough to get me to like the subject as much as many of my friends did. I enjoyed every other subject, but dreaded maths. I was okay at numbers but the harder the subject got, the less interested I became.

It didn't help that one of my close friends, Kylie, was a maths whiz. She was one of those students who always got full marks. A bad result for her was ninety-eight out of a hundred. When I reached high school, I found solace in a group of friends who also hated the subject and we'd wear the pitiful grades we got with pride. I stopped taking the subject seriously and would average twenty-eight out of a hundred in most tests. I was great at science and arts subjects but for reasons unexplained, logic wasn't my strongest asset at that age.

One day, a boy I had a crush on was moved into my maths class. Suddenly, my interest in this subject I'd barely bothered with went up. Not only was this boy in my class, he was also really good at the subject – annoyingly so. Just like Kylie.

One day after class, I noticed that he had stayed back to talk with some of the other students. So, as any reasonable teenager in my position would do, I came up with a plan that would hopefully increase my interaction with the cute boy and require minimal effort in applying my maths skills. I decided to use this opportunity after class to have a chat to him about music and about how great I thought the West Coast Eagles were (even though I was a staunch Fremantle Dockers supporter) and dazzle him with my personality. Then I could go back to not caring about maths.

The plan seemed to work. I'd spend a bit of time after every class joining in the post-maths class discussion with enthusiasm. It was all going well until one day, Cute Boy, feeling competitive after Kylie beat him in the last test, suggested that we, as a group of exceptional maths students, share our test scores after our next maths test to determine once and for all who the top student was. As far as they knew, I was just as good as any of them at the subject.

Panic kicked in and I suggested we all knew it was between him and Kylie because the teacher always announced the top scores to the class. Cute Boy disagreed, arguing that if we tallied the last few results and figured out the average, that would determine conclusively who was the better student. Everyone else seemed to agree and so there I was, terrified not only at the thought of having to sit a test I didn't want to, but also at the prospect of revealing my previous scores to this group who thought I was just as good at maths as they were.

As test day approached, I grew increasingly scared. I'd made good progress getting to know the cute boy and felt I was so close to him finally asking me out. I couldn't embarrass myself in front of him and everyone else in the group, so I thought up another plan. I knew it would take a miracle to raise my marks from averaging 30 per cent to 90 per cent in my next test. It would require a lot of study and I didn't have enough time. I thought I could fake an injury or, at the very least, cause slight injury to my arm so I would have to sit out the test.

I settled for the latter as my parents would cotton on to the fake injury and I'd get in trouble. I knew I was allergic to wasp stings and I also knew I wasn't allergic to bees, as they'd stung me before and they usually only left minor swelling. My plan required being around bees and they'd have to sting my right hand to ensure I was out of the game.

The morning of test day, I made my way to the park closest to my school in search of a bee colony. I knew that I'd been stung before on a hill while picking daisies. I decided to search for said hill, only to discover there weren't any daisies. I did notice a few bees hovering at the foot of the hill. I dropped my school bag and rolled down the hill, ensuring that my right hand was closest to the bees. Unfortunately, all this seemed to do was ward off the bees and ensure I was covered in grass stains. Just as I was getting up, I noticed a colony of bees swarming next to the tree above my head. I then flapped my right hand to ensure I was in their path, hoping I'd get stung. After what felt like an eternity of jumping up and down and waving my hand around, nothing happened.

Frustrated and running late for school, I picked up a branch and tried to knock the hive to force the bees to swarm out. Just as I was about to hit it, I felt a sharp pain on my hand – I had been stung. I felt very proud of myself and couldn't believe my genius plan had worked. As the pain intensified, I looked down at my hands, only to realise I had been stung on the wrong hand.

I walked to school and the nurse managed to remove the stinger and iced the swollen finger to help ease the pain. I hoped she'd see me suffering and send me home to rest up. Unfortunately, it wasn't enough to save me from sitting the test and she quickly ushered me out of her office, leaving me no option but to head to maths class. I took my seat and didn't speak to anyone, and avoided eye contact with Cute Boy. I hadn't planned on sitting the test, meaning I hadn't studied, and to this day cannot remember if I answered anything on the test paper.

When the class ended, I quickly ran out, and from then on avoided spending time with the group. Miraculously, the thought of being embarrassed in front of Cute Boy again forced me to try a little bit harder.

I did improve – slightly.

Bottomless

Alannah Hill

I WAS BORN WITHOUT a bottom.

I'll repeat that sentence. I was born *without* a bottom. Not a bottom to be seen. Not a bottom to be heard. Not a bottom to be ever spoken about. I was what is uncommonly referred to as 'Bottomless'.

For those unfamiliar with this scientific term, *bottomlessness* is, in fact, a rare, little-known condition that means one never, *ever* mentions their own bottoms, toilets or the bottoms of others. *Bottomlessness* is believed to be a Post Traumatic Stress Disorder response to repressed childhood memories so very gut-wrenching as to defy repression! My PTSD responses to bottoms, toilets and poo were set years earlier during my collapsible earthquake childhood in rural Tasmania.

To the outside world, I appeared to be growing up nicely in a run-down milk bar with my family in Penguin. But in reality, I was growing up rather *un*nicely in an abusive family that ignored me. The ruthless civil war of my parents' colossal marriage mistake had set brothers against brothers, sister against sister, parents against their own. My brothers ghosted through the milk bar's cramped quarters like three mysterious giants, no longer able to contain the anger and rage within. All three were possessed with secret powers I had little hope of attaining. My sister and I barely spoke, and my father was rarely home. My mother was always home – waiting for her prey.

We were instructed by our parents not to trust or talk to each other, and with their round-the-clock encouragement it *actually* worked. We discovered it was the *one* activity we did together really, *really* well. My mother's histrionic voice made me quake inside but I was bomb-struck by my father's apocalyptic moods.

Upon hearing my mother's shrill account of my father's impending arrival home, we all knew to run for the hills.

'Your FATHER'S home! Your FATHER'S HOME ... he's in the driveway, OH MY LORD ... somebody HELP me! Your FATHER is getting out of the car ... he's coming up the STEPS ... dear LORD ... he's WALKING in the door. Your FATHER is IN THE HOUSE. Your father's HOME!! Lanah, if you need to go to the toilet, go now! I'm timing you!'

Our toilet sat on four red bricks. The underside of the seat was stained a nasty dark yellow. I remember trying to wipe that stain away with bleach, metho and even turpentine, but nothing wiped that stain away. The toilet and four bricks sat on bug-infested seagrass matting, blackened with butted-out cigarettes and grey ash. The old-fashioned toilet chain was broken, which meant our toilet was often bogged. Toilet paper was scarce.

I remember listening to the despairing moans and bottomless grunts gasping for air from behind the toilet door. My father read the newspaper, smoked and hid in the toilet for up to three hours a day. My brothers smoked and flicked ash on the seagrass matting for up to two hours a day. My mum smoked and cried in the toilet when no one else was using it.

When I was a child my mum and Nan told me to keep *very* quiet whenever sitting on a toilet seat. 'God is watching you, Lanaaah! God can go *anywhere*! Just you remember, young lady, God is *everywhere*. He can see *everything* you're doing.'

I believed them.

I believed God could see through the toilet door. I believed he was watching every bad thing I did. It got so as I could barely breathe. And so, afraid to even move, often, I did nothing. I stopped eating food and lived on lollies. I was bottomless.

My mum took a spooky pride in nurturing my fear of all things 'toiletry'. She loved to sneak up on me, flick my loose pyjama bottoms, shriek and ask, 'How's ya *crack*, Lanaaaaaah? How's your *smelly* old *crack, dear?*'

If Mum saw my attempts to flee from the toilet arena, she'd quickly intervene, hands poised on hips. 'How did you GO IN there, dear? Have you got *untreatable* haemorrhoids, dear?'

Mum's fascination with bowels and bowel movements knew no limits. She believed that if you hadn't been given the gift of untreatable haemorrhoids, a prolapse, a nervous breakdown or chronic constipation by the time you were fifteen years old, you were simply … *not* living! One of Mum's happiest moments was when she told me about our neighbour Francine, who had *just* been admitted to the Burnie hospital with a case of untreatable haemorrhoids. Mum laughed for the first time in months when Francine told her they were the size of a bunch of grapes.

I stopped eating grapes and concentrated on my dream of becoming an international MTV star.

Paradoxically, the toilet was also my comfort place. A place I hid whenever I felt trouble looming. I learnt to cover my shut-up fear while I hid by cleaning that little throne of hell. Untoward, unrecognisable floating horrors were left drowning in the toilet bowl.

I always felt rather unwell in my stomach, but I persevered, and miraculously landed on a winning formula. I liked to call my winning formula Scoop and Throw. The untoward, unrecognisable horrors were thrown through the shattered windows. I'd watch them fall *disgracefully* onto the muddy lawn below. Nobody noticed I had created a home-made sewerage system. Sheets of heavy rain washed all the evidence away.

My bottomless fear of being shamed led to certain rules being established. Rules I lived by in order to live a normal life! Any talk of poo or vague acknowledgement that pooing might occur or had already occurred meant I had to leave any social situation in which I found myself. Pooing could not occur anywhere other than in my own home, with nobody else in the home but me. The term 'Bottoms up' did not register in my brain. I could not say the words 'toilet paper', let alone purchase it.

My carefully constructed faux-reality came crashing down one spring afternoon in September 1988, in a lavender and rose garden that lay hidden in the quiet, leafy suburb of East Malvern. I had been chosen by film director Richard Lowenstein, he of *Dogs in Space* infamy, to be the twirling dancing girl in a Crowded House video for their new single *Don't Dream It's Over*, a song of infinite tenderness, destined to become a global Number 1 hit. My razor-sharp girl-smarts knew this was going to be huge, and I dreamed of making my mark on the MTV media monolith through my twirling cat-moves.

In other words, I was moments away from becoming an *international* MTV star.

There was just one minor calamity. I had acquired a cinematic crush on the arty director. I wasn't sure if I had the skills to manage the conflicting emotions a cinematic crush requires. These kinds of situations usually ended up in a spectacular train wreck.

Thrilled and determined to do my best, I arrived at the video shoot wearing a lampshade as a fascinator on my wildly teased black hair. I gracefully tumbled forth, announcing, 'The character actress has *arrived!*'

The punky film crew sitting cross-legged on the ground didn't seem to notice my arrival. They were peering intently at a wall of sound amplifiers. Cool dulcet sounds drifted from the amplifiers, cool dulcet sounds I had never heard before. Apparently, the sounds belonged to a person called Eno.

Brian Eno.

I immediately noticed Victoria. Notoriously shy, sensible and intelligent, with the face of a Botticelli angel and a voice like the merest whisper of a kitten's meow, Victoria was the arty director's girlfriend. She watched me closely while whispering filmic truisms to her circle of admirers. I winked at her and she smiled shyly back. I was nervous, overdressed and intense. I hoped my post-Blitz make-up wasn't too blitzy for the Eno and Crowded House gang. I'd already prepared choreographed poses and was learning not to stare into the camera, Fellini style.

The director was waving his hands around and squinting into the sun. My unrequited crush on the arty director expanded, imploded and catastrophised, triggering the 1000-watt headlights of shame from my past.

The director approached me and flashed a flirtatious smile, asking if I felt comfortable twirling and whirling. Did I feel *comfortable* twirling around and around in a spooky, film-noir, slow-motion kind of way? *Sure* I did! I was *very* comfortable with that. I was moments away from becoming an international MTV star, after all.

But of course, I couldn't hear a word he said. My crush had suddenly made me deaf and mute, and what's more, I seemed to have shrunk. I felt only one inch tall. With the headlights of shame gathering force, I tried to make myself grow taller. As I spun through a number of practice twirls, I watched my crush stroking his girlfriend's hair, tenderly whispering into her ear and ignoring my twirling MTV dance moves.

At that moment, the producer announced loudly to the crew that my face would not be required for the video. Only my arty, dancing-girl body would be required.

The headlights of shame were shining their brightest glow towards me. I kidded myself that the cutting away from my face was because my white Marcel Marceau make-up was too bright for the screen. But deep within me, I believed the real reason was because I was too plain to be catapulted into people's lounge rooms on a Sunday evening at six o'clock for *Countdown*.

I knew the signs, but I didn't know the triggers. The familiar, sharp pains ringing the doorbell on every chamber in my museum of memories. It moved from door to door like a religious salesman, unwanted and unexpected.

I was desperate to find solitude. A place where I could hide for a little while, to hopefully regain my composure. (A common side-effect of childhood trauma is chronic stomach pains. Scientists believe stomach pains are linked to an unconscious clenching of the gut in response to repression.)

This is when I should have fled! But no ... I *continued* to twirl in my vintage 1940s frock, my head spinning like water down a drain pipe.

The memories of all my grand failures and insecurities sparked enough electricity to power a small country town.

Making excuses of 'freshening up', I grabbed my oversized pink bag and high heeled it across the lawn to the back door, and clawed my way up a carpeted Victorian staircase, stickybeaking at the dimly lit, run-down house – the rooms decorated in Bloomsbury style with oversized velvet lounging couches, Persian rugs, naive line drawings and ten curious house cats, twenty eyes watching my every stomach-churning step.

I kept my eyes fixed straight ahead.

The recovery room was almost in sight when disaster struck.

My cinematic crush, appearing out of nowhere, was standing at the top of the staircase. Crushes can do that – simply appear out of nowhere. Just like my father, hammering clenched fists on the toilet doors of my childhood, shouting, 'How bloody long are you going to be in there?' The director looked at me in a curious way, then handed me a bucket filled with water and said, 'You'll need this, love.'

His arty finger was on the PTSD trigger. I winced and attempted to look normal.

'Yeah,' he said, 'toilet's blocked. It's always bogging up. You'll need the water to flush everything down.'

Suddenly, I was twelve years old, hiding in the milk-bar toilet. I wanted to shout out that I was a bottomless person and wasn't going to use his blocked toilet anyway. A button had fallen off my dress and I could only sew it back on in the toilet. But I didn't say any of that. I was engaged in wilful denial. I slunk into the blocked toilet and quickly closed the door.

'All good in there, Alannah?' he called out. I could see the tips of his boots through the crack under the door, work boots just like my father's.

Darkness had engulfed the small room, silence filled the air. My eyes flickered in time to a marching-girl heartbeat.

And then I saw it. I smelt it. I panicked. I recoiled so fast that I fell against the toilet door. Something was floating in the toilet bowl. The fog of horror from one of my brothers' monster droppings floated before my eyes. I knew this ghastly intruder had nothing to do with me and *everything* to do with *somebody* else.

What the *hell* was I going to do? The dulcet sounds of Eno floated up from the garden as I pulled on the wretched chain. I quickly calculated I had enough water in the bucket for only one flush. My stomach was churning. I heard my crush's boots going down the stairs. Time was running out.

Giving it one shot, I held my breath and poured the water into the bowl, praying for a miracle. Go down! Go down that toilet bowl, I pleaded. Go DOWN. I watched the flush coming to an end, but it refused to go down. Too big for rusted Victorian pipes.

'Alaaaaarnnaaaaar?' the director called out playfully from somewhere. 'You need a hand?'

All my twelve-year-old smarts kicked in. Everything was crystal clear. I did what *any* bottomless girl would do when forced into a corner – destroy *all* evidence. I wrapped my frail, white hands in layers of soft embossed toilet paper, scooped the devil's fruit from its swampy lair, then carefully swaddled it in freshly prepared toilet paper.

I heard a noise on the stairs.

'Hey, Alannah ... Is the toilet leaking?'

It was God. He was watching.

I climbed up onto the toilet seat and peered out the small window above. In the distance, I could see magnificent trees, their branches swaying in time to the twirling, swirling rhythms of my bottomless mind. My throw needed to hold all the mighty girl-force of my skilful basketball days. I was Diana with her hunting bow, dispensing what I'd found in the toilet with clear, controlled composure. Then I aimed that package with as much force behind it as any Penguin State School basketball player could muster. I threw that package of shame far, far away, into another world and dimension. Far away into the distant majestic trees.

Or so I thought.

I heard a voice yelling from below, 'Hey! What the fu—!'

Fragments of the bomb were gliding through the air like a confetti explosion at a wedding. My triple-wrapped package in embossed toilet paper had bottomed out in mid-air and burst open with almighty gusto. My heart was now outside my body as the bomb of shame splattered across the feet of the entire crew. I watched it fall onto lilac rose bushes and into beds of bright yellow daffodils. Someone complained she'd found fragments in her hair. I looked down as the director looked up, his face a misery of confusion.

And then the rest of the film crew, Victoria, the director of photography, and the fresh-faced members of Crowded House all looked up as one, just in time to see my face, a shrieking gargoyle sitting atop the Notre Dame cathedral.

I cannot *quite* recall what happened next. I remember the shameful memories I associate with an entirely different person, the old Alannah. I remember feeling like someone had suddenly turned a heater on inside my body, and my skin turning from white to beetroot.

I clambered down from the black toilet seat, grabbed my pink bag and ran to the safety of my car. I found the keys, turned the ignition and pushed the shame away with very loud music.

I never looked back.

There are times, dear reader, when I feel it's important *not* to look back. Deep shame flourishes in the darkness, pedalling away at our very core.

We try to overcome shame by demanding to speak to the little child who still exists within us. This little hide and seek child can be hard to find. I reached out to my little Alannah squatting on a stained potty in the deep south of Tasmania. I was struggling to understand what I was meant to do. Little Alannah looked up at me with a pained bottomless expression. She waved her little hands in the air and told me to write a note to myself every morning. She told me to write: 'Deep shame isn't real, and it wasn't my fault.'

And as I walked away from little Alannah squatting on her stained potty, in the deep south of Tasmania, she turned her head toward the sun, pointed her finger and said, 'Alannah! *If it* IS *your* fault, make *sure* you get rid of all the evidence.'

Fireworks in Beirut

Jan Fran

IN HINDSIGHT I should never have had my colon cleansed in Lebanon. But then everything is so much clearer in hindsight, isn't it? If I'm being honest, it should have been clear back then, but I was twenty-two and had just spent eight weeks traipsing around Europe, subsisting solely on a diet of packet gorgonzola and warm 4 euro vodka. And in case you're wondering, yes, I did lug a 1.25-litre glass bottle of 4 euro vodka in a roller bag across several European state boundaries.

My sabbatical was to conclude at the home of my uncle George, on the Mediterranean's twenty-seventh best island, Cyprus. Little did I know when he picked me up from Nicosia airport that balmy August afternoon that Cyprus was not to be my final destination.

My father's brother George – much like my father – had left Lebanon in search of a better life. Unlike my father, he found it a mere 246 kilometres away in Cyprus. George is a very nice man who also happens to be riddled with guilt at being an absentee godfather to the one niece entrusted to his care in the eyes of God: me. That might go some way towards explaining why, when I casually mentioned feeling tired and sluggish, he wildly overcompensated and suggested flying us both to Lebanon to meet with what he described as an 'excellent natural doctor'.

'How do you know this doctor?' I inquired.

'I saw him on the TV!'

Excellent!

Now, as Australians, our sense of distance is warped by the fact that we inhabit the world's sixth largest country and if you live on the east coast, it's easier to get to Indonesia than it is to get to Perth. Our friends in the correct-side-up hemisphere can spend an hour on a plane and end up on another continent entirely. In our case it was forty minutes.

Beirut felt like it could explode at any time, either with celebratory fireworks or with the slightly more menacing kind – a fact that appeared to perturb no one.

The 'excellent natural doctor' we had come to see was waiting for us in an obnoxiously well-lit clinic. He greeted us at the reception desk and we made the obligatory small talk about Australia before he showed us to his surgery.

'What's the problem?' he asked as we took our seats.

'Well,' I said in a form of Arabic that sounded like it came from a monkey with a brain injury. 'I'm very tired and … and …'

I searched for the word 'sluggish' to no avail.

Uncle George interrupted. 'She's been travelling all over Europe and she's very tired and bloated. Can you help her?'

The excellent natural doctor ignored me. 'Yes! We help tired and bloated people all the time,' he said brightly.

He walked over to a small mahogany cupboard and pulled out several plastic mason jars with bright yellow labels.

'Take two of these, one of these, three of these, one of these and two of these a day.'

He sensed my apprehension. 'Don't worry,' he assured me. 'They're only herbs. If you eat well and drink lots of water, in six weeks you won't be tired or bloated anymore.'

I held one of the capsules up to the light. It was indeed filled with what looked like finely ground herbs.

'Great,' exclaimed my uncle. We stood up to leave.

'There is one more thing you could do,' said the excellent natural doctor.

'Yes.'

'Have you ever thought about cleansing your colon?'

'My colon?'

'Your colon.'

Friends, I had literally *never* thought about my colon, let alone the cleansing of it. I wasn't even sure where my colon was or what it did, and I certainly didn't know how to cleanse it.

'Her colon could probably use a cleanse,' chimed Uncle George.

'Yes, probably,' concurred the excellent natural doctor. 'It'll take a few minutes and you'll feel immediately better.'

I sat in my seat, quietly taking umbrage at the two men swapping notes about the state of my colon until finally it was decided I would have my colon cleansed and my uncle would foot the bill.

'Fine!' I was too tired and bloated to argue.

Dear readers, this is the part where I insist you don't feel sorry for me in any way because I had ample opportunities to twig to what was about to happen to me ... and I didn't! Not when I was led into a small room complete with an examination table and various other medical paraphernalia; not when I was told to take off my knickers and put on a hospital gown, making sure to leave open the slit at the back; not even when the excellent natural doctor insisted it wouldn't hurt. At no point did I conclude that in a few moments I would be *literally* shitting myself.

That moment finally came when I spotted a spritely, middle-aged woman with unreasonably long fingernails generously applying lubricant to a long plastic tube, the other end of which was attached to a small, unfamiliar machine that was gently humming in the corner of the room.

'What's this tube for?' I asked.

She laughed, then stopped abruptly once she realised I was serious. 'It's for your colon cleanse.'

Sometimes in moments of intense trauma we see our lives flash before our eyes. I only saw the rudimentary anatomy chart that hung on the wall of my grade 3 classroom as my mind desperately scanned itself for any information it may have retained about colons. Colons are associated with poop and poop is associated with butts and butts are associated with lube and lubes are associated with tubes and tubes …

The colour drained from my face.

Sensing my distress, the long-fingernailed woman, whose name I later found out was Gina, offered some calming words. 'Once this tube is in there, you won't feel a thing.'

For those who've never had a colon cleanse (also known as a colonic irrigation or colonic hydrotherapy for the more posh among us), congratulations, you've made a sage life choice. The rest of us would know that a tube goes in your butt, water goes up the tube, poop comes down. Rinse and repeat.

'My daughter loves Australia,' said Gina casually, inserting the tube into my butt. I winced! She began massaging my stomach with a vibrating gadget akin to an ultrasound probe.

'It helps get things moving.' She winked.

I pursed my lips.

'Is it hot in Australia?'

'Umm … yeah it can be.'

'Do you have sharks in Australia?'

'Yup. We have sharks.'

'Have you seen a shark?'

'Nope!'

'I don't think I'd want to see a shark.'

I didn't answer. There's something disconcerting about making small talk with a stranger as they evacuate your bowels.

After exhausting all Australia-related topics of conversation we moved on to Lebanon, which proved an avenue for Gina to vent about corrupt government officials and how none of the public amenities functioned properly.

'We're almost there,' Gina assured me, sensing my restlessness.

Lebanon has a funny way of pipping you at the post. My cousin Zee used to say that Lebanon is full of action – which kind, however, he'd neglected to specify. You never really knew what fireworks you were going to get, but somehow you knew they were coming.

The unfamiliar machine attached to the other end of my plastic butt tube, which had been gently humming in the corner of the room, suddenly started to splutter before shutting down entirely. The lights above us began flickering, the sound of static interrupted the dull rumble of medical equipment, and the room suddenly went dark.

'W… what's going on?' I stammered. I wanted to get up but was somewhat restricted by the plastic tube poking out of my butt.

Gina looked concerned. She called out to her colleague in the adjacent room. 'Samir!'

Elevated voices. Brisk footsteps. Clanging.

'Let me find out what's going on,' she said, removing her rubber gloves.

'Wait!' I stammered, my neck straining. 'You can't just leave me here.'

'You'll be fine.'

'What if it's, like, an *attack*?' I'm often the first to scold Australians who jump to defamatory conclusions about Lebanon based solely on what they see on the news and yet there I was, Lebanese and a journalist no less, quite certain of imminent war because I'd heard a commotion in a hallway. I looked at Gina, waiting for her to reassure me that it was no such thing.

'It could be.' She shrugged. 'I'll be right back. Just stay very still, otherwise you'll …' she gestured with her arms. 'Well, you know, you'll make a mess.'

I tried to gather my thoughts. Here I was on a gurney, with a plastic tube in my arse, literally shitting myself in the middle of an attack on Beirut. Is this how it would end for Jeannette Francis? In that moment I thought about my uncle George and the great irony that his desire to be a good godfather ultimately killed his niece. I was too scared to even cross myself lest the movement of my arms inadvertently bumped the plastic tube that suddenly felt only tenuously in place. The commotion in the hallway intensified. If I wasn't sure whether Beirut was under attack before, I certainly was now. My mind spun! It was Hezbollah; no, it was Israel; no, it was Syria; no, it was the Ottomans! I thought of the authorities eventually finding my body among the rubble, exposed from the waist down with a plastic tube stuck up my arse. I imagined that image on the news being beamed into homes all over the world. 'Is that Jan from school being pulled from rubble in Beirut with a tube up her arse?' Yes, this was how it would end for Jeannette Francis. My heart began to pound and I could feel the tears coming. I closed my eyes and tried to drown my thoughts out with a silent prayer.

'Dear God, please don't let me die like this,' I pleaded.

Suddenly, as if by the hand of God herself, the lights came on again. The unfamiliar machine that had spluttered off came back to life and resumed its gentle humming as though nothing had happened. The rest of the machines in the room started whirring and beeping as they had before. The elevated voices hushed. The brisk footsteps slowed. The clanging stopped. Gina flitted into the room, slipped on a new pair of rubber gloves and resumed her seat at my bedside, inspecting the plastic tube with her eyes.

'You moved!' she scolded me.

I stared at her with my mouth open.

'Not to worry,' she continued, popping the plastic tube out from inside my butt. 'You're all done anyway.' I had no more shits left to give.

'What the hell happened?'

'With what?'

I started at her, incredulous.

'With the … the *thing* …' I gestured at the lights with my eyes, still too traumatised to move.

'Oh, the electricity cut out, that's all!'

'That's *all?*'

'It's Lebanon, darling,' she said. 'I told you, nothing works properly. It happens all the time. That's why we have generators. How do you feel after that, good?'

I blinked silently at her.

I was led out to the reception area where Uncle George was waiting for me.

'How was that?' he asked.

'Fine,' I said eventually.

'Great. Let's get some lunch. You're probably hungry after shitting yourself in there,' he joked.

If only he knew.

Gorilla and the Bird

Zack McDermott

W HEN THE POLICE found me, I was standing on a subway platform somewhere in Brooklyn. I was shirtless. I was barefoot. I was freezing. I was crying. I'd spent the previous ten hours wandering through the streets of New York, convinced that I was being video-taped, *Truman Show* style, by my stand-up comedy partner.

As soon as I walked out of my apartment that afternoon, I knew the cameras were rolling. The people on the streets looked like the normal East Village crowd, but they were all archetypes. The skaters were all wearing the same DC brand shoes. Everyone was wearing the same expensive skinny Levis. The construction workers' accents were a little too Brooklyn thick and their boots a little too perfectly well worn not to be plants. Even the heroin addicts were too pretty. When I looked really close I could see that their face tattoos were actually professional make-up jobs.

That all made sense to me. I was a public defender. That's how I made my living, representing indigent and frequently mentally ill clients. But at night I'd been doing stand-up. And I was convinced that my partner, who had Hollywood connections, had arranged to have me filmed without me knowing because he knew I wasn't an actor, so it would be more natural.

I was thrilled. The whole city of New York was my set.

I sprinted to the park at the end of my block. I was amazed at how well they'd cast 'generic old man on park bench'. He was old, he had a bicycle. He was too old to have a bicycle. I went up to him (by the way I had a Mohawk) and said, 'Hello.' He nervously returned the greeting and I grabbed his bike with the intention of taking a few laps around the block.

The old man said, 'No!' The old man had some chops. So, knowing our scene was up, I sprinted to the dog park. I hurdled the fence and before popping out the other side, I dropped down on all fours to gallop with the pack a little bit, giving the people what they wanted.

At the end of the dog run, I saw rec league soccer players kicking the ball around, warming up as the game was about to start. Perfect. I'd played soccer in college. I ushered the keeper aside, got between the sticks and started yelling at the strikers. They started shooting. I saved everything. I welcomed the keeper back in the box after a few saves. 'That's how it's done, son, now get back between the pipes and keep clean.'

Then, from across the field I heard, 'Get the fuck off the field!'

I yell back, 'Who me? Fuck you.'

I pulled down my shorts and started sprinting in and around the pitch for the entirety of the first half, butt cheeks flapping in the wind. Once I was satisfied we had what we needed, I sprinted across First Avenue and Halston, one of the busier intersections in downtown Manhattan, taxi drivers breaking and screeching and swerving around me while yelling a variety of obscenities. I knew I was all right, though. I knew these were professional stunt drivers on a closed set, so nothing bad could come to me.

On the other side of Halston and First Avenue, a group of young African American men were standing in a circle, drinking beers and smoking and shooting the shit. I took that opportunity to unilaterally engage them in a rap battle.

A bomb atomically, Socrates, philosophies and hypotheses

Can't define how I will be dropping these mockeries lyrically performed armed robberies flee with the lottery

Possibly they spot 'em battle scared Shogun explosion where my pen hits
Tremendous Ultraviolent shine blind forensics!

I won.

The guy who seemed to be the leader said, 'You crazy, man, you should roll.'

I rolled.

Minutes later I was on a Brooklyn-bound L train. I'd lost my shoes and shirt along the way, and I started doing pull-ups on the overhead bar, thinking, this is going to be great for promos and B-roll.

The train stopped. Everybody spilled out in their own direction; half went left, half went right, and I didn't know who to follow. I'd lost the game. I started crying so hard my contacts flushed out of my eyes. I held my hands up like a captured soldier. And ready for my close-up. That's when the NYPD walked up. Their uniforms looked real.

First cop asked me, 'What's the matter, buddy?'

'I don't know.'

'You've got no shirt on, you've got no shoes on and you are crying, that don't seem like a problem to you?'

'I think the problem is I am cold.'

They cuffed me for safety purposes, and instead of finding myself in the back of a squad car I found myself in the back of an ambulance. After a couple of minutes, the radio crackled on. 'Intake available at Bellevue psych ward.'

Cut to psych ward. Interior, day.

Patients were pacing the ward like drugged-up zombies. People were howling. People were screaming. People were fighting. People were tackled, injected, placed in secluded rubber rooms. The place looked exactly like the set in *One Flew Over the Cuckoo's Nest*, except no one was smoking. For all I knew we'd secured permission to shoot there.

At the end of that first afternoon I was pulled out of my zombie-like trance when I heard, 'McDermott, visitor.'

That was the first time I'd heard the word 'visitor' since I'd been there. Standing on the other side of the locked doors was a fifty-year-old woman who looked a great deal like my mother, The Bird. I'd nicknamed my mother 'The Bird' when I was in high school because she has a rather large bosom and when she gets excited, about things good or bad, she tends to jerk her head around. And she has a big nose. Kinda like mine. She calls me 'The Gorilla'.

She walked through the doors that said, 'Danger of Patient Elopement', past some nylon restraints, and she looked at me and said, 'You're a bag of bones, Gorilla.'

I said, 'Bird?'

She said, 'The Bird is here.'

I said, 'The Bird can't be here. She lives in Kansas.'

She said, 'The Bird got on a plane. What are you doing here?'

They escorted us to the cafeteria that doubles as the visitors' room. Mom calmly tried to explain to me that she'd been to my apartment and seen that I'd drawn over every inch of the walls with a red Sharpie pen.

'Zack, you are in a locked psychiatric ward,' she told me.

'Mom, you are a terrible actor,' I told her.

For the next ten days, she was outside those 'Danger of Patient Elopement' doors twenty minutes before visiting hours started, twice a day, and she stayed until they kicked her out. Eventually, due to a heavy dose of anti-psychotic medication, coupled with a heavy dose of The Bird's calming reassurance that this was real, the cinematic dissolved into reality and I realised, as quickly as catching a cold, that I had lost my mind.

I went back to Wichita, Kansas, with my mom and for the next ninety days I smoked and drank my face off in her garage. She filled prescriptions for me. I lost my hair, I became impotent, I gained thirty pounds. And then my disability pay ran out. I had to go back to New York. I had to go back to work.

I began public defending again. Same clientele. All indigent, none who could afford a lawyer, many mentally ill. And every time I was forced to send someone to a psych ward, it tore me in half because I knew more than I ever cared to know about where I was sending them.

I'm all right. I wrote a book. I knew I was never going to end up on a park bench shouting at pigeons. I have health insurance. I have a JD. My mom has a PhD. I have friends whose parents are psychiatrists. I wasn't going to be the guy who falls through the cracks. But so many do.

Now my mom, she lives by this philosophy that when people are at their worst, when you are repelled by them and when every instinct you have is to run, what you really need to do is go towards them.

I'm a gorilla. I'm a bi-polar gorilla. I am also a bird.

Be a gorilla when you have to be. Be a bird when you can.

And go towards each other.

Meet the Catastrophisers

ALANNAH HILL is one of Australia's most loved fashion designers and author of the bestselling memoir *Butterfly on a Pin*. In 2013, at the height of her trailblazing success, Alannah famously parted ways with Factory X, her financial backers, sending shock waves through the fashion industry. In 2014, with her typical all-or-nothing drive, Alannah launched her new brand, Louise Love, sold exclusively to David Jones and online. After a melanoma scare in 2016, Alannah threw herself into writing *Butterfly on a Pin*, the startling, harrowing and shocking story of her life. Alannah lives in Melbourne with her son, Edward.

ANDREW P. STREET is a Sydney-built, Adelaide-based author, journalist, commentator and failed indie rock star. He's written for pretty much everyone at one time or another, as well as three books, including the bestselling *The Short and Excruciatingly Embarrassing Reign of Captain Abbott*, and is currently senior writer for *GOAT*.

ANNABEL CRABB is a Sydney-based ABC writer and presenter. After the birth of her first child, as outlined in this book, her enthusiasm was sufficiently undimmed to have two more. During her working hours, Annabel writes for the ABC about politics and social issues, and presents TV shows including *Kitchen Cabinet*, *The House with Annabel Crabb*, *Back in Time for Dinner* and *Tomorrow Tonight*. She is a recidivist author whose latest work is a cookbook with childhood friend Wendy Sharpe. Annabel co-presents the podcast *Chat 10 Looks 3* with colleague and friend Leigh Sales.

ANNIE NOLAN is the media personality behind the popular blog *Uncanny Annie*. Since starting her blog in 2015 Annie has gained a following across various social media platforms, where she freely shares her life experience and opinions on important social issues, mixed in with a healthy dose of kids, animals, glitter and weirdness. Some of the causes Annie is passionate about include gender equality, LGBTQI rights, Aboriginal rights, environmentalism and animal welfare. Annie lives in Melbourne with her husband, Western Bulldogs AFL player Liam Picken, her three children and all the animals she can adopt. She also co-hosts a podcast with Bianka Thompson called *We Want to be Better*.

BERNARD SALT AM is a columnist with *The Australian* newspaper. He is also now the managing director of the speaking and advisory firm The Demographics Group, following a long career as a partner in a global corporate advisory firm. He has written six books, is a regular on the Australian corporate speaking circuit, and is an adjunct professor at Curtin University Business School. In 2017 he was made a Member of the Order of Australia (AM). Bernard also single-handedly, and quite inadvertently, popularised the term 'smashed avocado' globally.

CATHY WILCOX is a cartoonist for the *Sydney Morning Herald* and *The Age*, for which she has drawn since 1989, collecting three Walkley Awards for her work along the way. She is the mother of two mostly grown-up children and one eternally childlike dog. She lives in Sydney.

CLEM BASTOW is a screenwriter and award-winning cultural critic. Her work appears regularly in *The Saturday Paper* and *The Guardian*, and she has written for journals, including *The Lifted Brow* and *Kill Your Darlings*, and books, including *Copyfight* (NewSouth Publishing, 2015) and the upcoming *ReFocus: The Films of Elaine May* (Edinburgh University Press). In 2017 she wrote and co-presented the ABC podcast *Behind the Belt*, a documentary 'deep dive' into professional wrestling. She holds a Master of Screenwriting from VCA, teaches screenwriting at the University of Melbourne, and is currently undertaking a PhD in action cinema and screenwriting.

DEBORAH KNIGHT began her career in radio working for Mix 106.5 in Sydney and for Triple J. Moving to television, she was a presenter–reporter with the ABC's *Landline*, and then a journalist in the Canberra Press Gallery for Network Ten, going on to head up Ten's US Bureau, covering such stories as September 11 and the Iraq War. Renowned for her journalistic skills, Deborah moved to the Nine Network in 2011, where she hosted and co-hosted *Financial Review Sunday*, *Weekend Today* and *A Current Affair*. She now presents *The Today* Show with Georgie Gardner. Deborah and her husband, Lindsay, have three children.

EMMA ALBERICI is the Chief Economics Correspondent for the ABC. Until 2017 she was the presenter of the ABC's flagship news and current affairs program *Lateline*. She has worked as the finance editor for the ABC's *7.30* and as a reporter for radio current affairs programs *AM*, *PM* and *The World Today*. Between 2008 and 2012, during the height of the global financial crisis, Emma was the ABC's Europe Correspondent based in London. She was a reporter and producer with *A Current Affair*, *Business Sunday* and *The Today Show* on Australia's Nine Network. She has written three business books and has been a finalist three times in the Walkley Awards.

ESTELLE TANG is a senior editor at ELLE.com, where she interviews celebrities and sometimes dresses up like them. She was once asked if her life was like the movie *How to Lose a Guy in 10 Days*, and the answer was not 'No'. She was previously a literary scout, a textbook wrangler, and a contributor at Rookie. She has written reviews and essays for the *Guardian*, *Jezebel*, *The Age*, *The Australian*, *NewYorker.com*, *Pitchfork*, *frankie*, *Meanjin*, *Kill Your Darlings* and *Australian Book Review*. Estelle lives in Brooklyn, New York.

FRANK MOORHOUSE has won major national literary prizes for his novels, short stories and essays. He is best known for the highly acclaimed Edith trilogy, *Grand Days*, *Dark Palace* and *Cold Light* novels, which follow the career of an Australian woman struggling to become a diplomat in the 1920s and 1930s through to the 1970s. His most recent book, *The Drover's Wife* (Penguin Random House, 2018), brings together works inspired by Henry Lawson's story and Russell Drysdale's painting of the same name. He was made a Member of the Order of Australia in 1985 and a Doctor of Letters by the University of Sydney in 2015.

IVAN COYOTE, born and raised in Whitehorse, Yukon, Canada, is a writer and storyteller. The author of twelve books, the creator of four films, six stage shows and three albums that combine storytelling with music, in 2019 Ivan will mark twenty-five years on the road as an internationally touring storyteller and musician. Coyote's new book, *ReBent Sinner*, will be released in 2019 with Arsenal Pulp Press. In 2017, Ivan was awarded an honorary PhD from Simon Fraser University, Canada, for writing and activism.

JAMES JEFFREY is the award-winning parliamentary sketch-writer and Strewth columnist for *The Australian*. His latest book is *The Wonks's Dictionary* (MUP), co-created with cartoonist Jon Kudelka. He is also the author of *My Family and Other Animus* (MUP, 2018) and *Paprika Paradise* (Hachette Australia, 2007).

JAN FRAN is a journalist, TV presenter and online commentator. She is best known for hosting *The Feed* on SBS Viceland and creating *The Frant,* where she dissects the daily news online, and as guest-host on Network Ten's *The Project*. She speaks three languages, has lived in Lebanon, France, Bangladesh and Uganda, and has shot and produced international documentaries for SBS. A social commentator on Sky News and the ABC, she was a finalist for Best Television Personality in *Cosmo*'s Woman of the Year Award and for the 2018 Walkley for Women's Leadership in Media. Jan is a Plan International ambassador, advocating for women and girls.

JENNY VALENTISH is well-accustomed to catastrophe, so much so that she has dedicated three books to the topic: the anthology *Your Mother Would Be Proud*, the novel *Cherry Bomb*, and the non-fiction book *Woman of Substances: A Journey into Addiction and Treatment*. Jenny is a journalist who writes for the *Sydney Morning Herald*, *The Age*,

The Saturday Paper, *The Guardian* and *The Monthly*. She lives and works on Dja Dja Wurrung land.

JEREMY FERNANDEZ is a journalist, producer and presenter with the ABC. He has anchored and reported in the field for some of the network's most complex broadcasts, including state and federal elections and budgets, the Brexit referendum, the Anzac and Remembrance Day centenaries, Sydney's Martin Place siege, Melbourne's Commonwealth Games and Perth's Claremont serial killer investigation. He has also hosted the Australian of the Year Awards and the Australian Human Rights Commission's annual awards ceremony. Jeremy has previously worked with CNN, News International and the Seven Network. He was born to an Indian family in Kuala Lumpur, and has since lived and worked in Perth, Melbourne, London and Sydney.

JUANITA PHILLIPS is a writer and broadcaster who presents the ABC TV's 7 pm news bulletin in New South Wales. She started in journalism nearly forty years ago, bashing out newspaper stories on a manual typewriter, before moving into television. Juanita has worked in London for the BBC and in the US for CNN International, written children's books and a memoir called *A Pressure Cooker Saved My Life*. She tweets about life as a single mother to Boy Teen and Girl Teen.

KATE MCCLYMONT is an investigative journalist with the *Sydney Morning Herald* and a seven-time Walkley Award winner, including the Gold Walkley. She was named the 2012 NSW Journalist of the Year for her investigations into the head of the Health Services Union, and the business activities of Eddie Obeid. McClymont is also the recipient of numerous other awards including the Australian Shareholders' Association Award for excellence in financial reporting, and the NSW Law Society's Golden Quill Award for excellence in legal reporting (1990 and 1992). In 2017, she was inducted into the Media Hall of Fame. With Linton Besser, she published *He Who Must Be Obeid*, which chronicles corruption in NSW. She is currently the Pro-Chancellor at the University of Sydney and a Fellow of the Senate.

KIRSTIE CLEMENTS is an author, journalist, speaker and former editor-in-chief (1999–2012) of *Vogue Australia*. Her memoir of three decades in fashion publishing, *The Vogue Factor* (MUP 2013), was published in seven countries, followed by a behind-the-scenes novella, *Tongue in Chic* (MUP 2014), and *Impressive: How to Have a Stylish Career* (MUP 2015). She has also co-authored two illustrated books on fashion, *In Vogue: 50 Years of Australian Style* (HarperCollins 2009) and *The Australian Women's Weekly Fashion: The First 50 Years* (2014) for the National Library of Australia.

LARISSA BEHRENDT is the Distinguished Professor at the University of Technology, Sydney and Director of Research and Academic Programs, Jumbunna Institute of Indigenous Education and Research. Her novel *Home* won the 2002 David Uniapon Award and a 2005 Commonwealth Writer's Prize, and her second novel, *Legacy*, won a Victorian Premier's Literary Award. Larissa's most recent book is *Finding Eliza*. She hosts ABC Radio's *Speaking Out*; wrote and directed the feature films *After the Apology* and *Innocence Betrayed*; has written and produced several short films; and won the 2018 Australian Directors Guild Award for Best Direction in a Feature Documentary. Larissa was awarded the 2009 NAIDOC Person of the Year Award and 2011 NSW Australian of the Year.

MARC FENNELL, interviewer, author, journalist and presenter, has hosted the ABC podcast *Download This Show* since 2012, and is regularly on ABC Radio Sydney. He is also the co-anchor of SBS's current-affairs program *The Feed*. Marc has worked with the BBC, Triple J, Network Ten, Showtime, Foxtel, Monocle, Fairfax, Junkee, the Sydney Opera House and Red Bull. Based in Sydney, he has reported across the USA, UK, France and Asia. He has written two books, *That Movie Book* (HarperCollins, 2011) and *Planet According to the Movies* (HarperCollins, 2016), and created the 2019 Audible Originals series *It Burns*. Marc is the Creative Director of the not-for-profit group Media Diversity Australia.

RICHARD GLOVER is the author of a weekly humour column that has been published in the *Sydney Morning Herald* for more than twenty years. He also writes regularly for *The Washington Post*, and presents the top-rating *Drive* show on ABC Radio in Sydney. In December 2011, he and Peter Fitzsimons achieved a record for the world's longest radio interview, supervised by the Guinness Book of Records. Richard is the author of numerous books including *Flesh Wounds* (HarperCollins, 2015) and *The Land Before Avocado* (HarperCollins, 2018).

RICK MORTON, an author and award-winning reporter, has covered social policy for *The Australian* since 2013. He also writes a column in *The Weekend Australian*'s 'Review' section. Rick is the author of *One Hundred Years of Dirt* (MUP, 2018), a family memoir about trauma, poverty and the isolation of the Queensland outback. And he once almost found a dinosaur.

ROBBIE BUCK is a broadcaster on ABC Radio Sydney. He sets his alarm for an ungodly hour and co-hosts *Breakfast* with Wendy Harmer. He began his broadcasting career at the ripe old age of ten, when he was introduced to community radio in Lismore. For the past two decades he's presented programs across the gamut of the broadcast spectrum. He's well known for his thirteen-year stint hosting for the Australian youth broadcasting network Triple J. Robbie lives in Sydney with his wife and two children, and continues to pursue his love of music and photography.

SALLY RUGG is an LGBTQI activist and Executive Director of Change.org. As Campaign Director and Creative Director at GetUp, 2013–2018, she worked at the forefront of Australia's marriage equality campaign. In 2018, Sally received the Fbi Radio SMAC of the Year Award; was named Pedestrian.tv's Strayan of the Year; and was a Hero of the Year finalist at the Australian LGBTI Awards. In 2017, she was named among *Harper's Bazaar*'s Five Women of the Year; by *Cosmopolitan* magazine as one of Australia's Most Influential LGBTQI people; Amnesty International's Top 15 Women Championing Human Rights in Australia; and topped Mamamia's Most Powerful LGBTQI Women list. Sally's first book, *How Powerful We Are* (Hachette Australia, 2019), will tell the real story of how Australia got marriage equality.

SANTILLA CHINGAIPE is an award-winning journalist and filmmaker. Working for SBS *World News* for nearly a decade, she reported from across Africa and interviewed some of the continent's most prominent leaders. She created and curated the *Africa Talks* series, and Australia's first all-day, anti-racism festival, *Not Racist, But ...* in partnership with the Wheeler Centre, Melbourne. She also founded the annual *Behind the Screens* initiative, which aims to increase the representation of people from underrepresented groups in the Australian screen industry. Her latest film, *Black As Me*, explores perceptions of beauty and race in Australia. She writes for *The Saturday Paper* and is a member of the federal government's Advisory Group on Australia–Africa Relations.

STEVE LUCAS is best known as frontman for seminal punk band X and gained notoriety as lead singer for hard-rocking outfit Bigger Than Jesus. Hailed as a 'Living Legend' by *Australia's Rolling Stone*, and as 'The Elderly Stateman of Rock and Roll', he has toured as far afield as Nepal and the USA. Steve's solo career has extended more than forty years, and he still plays regularly with blues-based band The Heinous Hounds. His music has been included in TV series and films such as *The Idiot Box* and *The Boys*, and he has guested on Rockwizz and hosted RAGE. Steve is known for his charitable works raising money and awareness for the prevention of child sex abuse and exploitation. He is happily married to Joey Bedlam, with whom he collaborates on music projects with artists from all over the world.

SUSAN CARLAND is an Australian academic, author and social commentator. She is the director of the Bachelor of Global Studies at Monash University, the same university from which she received her PhD in Sociology. She is the host of SBS's *Child Genius*, and author of *Fighting Hislam: Women, faith and sexism* (MUP, 2017). Susan is an ambassador for the Asylum Seeker Resource Centre, and also a certified scuba diver.

WENDY HARMER, in a career spanning four decades, has found success as a journalist, columnist, radio broadcaster, TV host, author, playwright and comic performer. A former political journalist, Wendy forged a career in comedy in the 1980s at the Edinburgh Festival, London's West End and on stages in Ireland, the US and all over Australia. She has been a pioneer for women in media as MC of ABC TV's *The Big Gig*, headliner in radio 2Day FM's *Morning Crew*, and as the first female host of the *Logies* TV awards, in 2002. The author of some thirty books, she has also written plays, an opera libretto and been a columnist for many magazines and newspapers. These days she is co-host of ABC Sydney's *Breakfast* with Robbie Buck. Wendy is married to Brendan Donohoe, they have two children and live on Sydney's Northern Beaches.

ZACK MCDERMOTT is the author of *Gorilla and the Bird: A Memoir of Madness and a Mother's Love.* He worked as a public defender for the Legal Aid Society of New York for six years. His work has appeared in the *New York Times*, *This American Life*, *Morning Edition*, *Gawker*, *Deadspin* and *SplitSider*, among others. He is from Wichita, Kansas, and is a graduate of the University of Kansas and the University of Virginia School of Law. Zack lives in New York and Los Angeles.

Acknowledgements

WE'D LIKE TO thank Julian Morrow for supporting the idea of *The Full Catastrophe* as a live show and podcast, which has led to this book. And the great team at Giant Dwarf, especially Nikita Agzarian, Dave Harmon, Bryce Halliday and Beth McMullen.

Thanks to all the generous storytellers and writers. We owe you all a gin and tonic.

Thanks to our agent, Jeanne Ryckmans, from Camerons Management.

Thanks to our kids – Georgie, Gus, Sofia, Sadie and Stella.

And thanks to the wonderful women at Hardie Grant for believing in this project so much, Arwen Summers, Marg Bowman and Bernadette Foley.

The story *Gorilla and the Bird* by Zack McDermott was drawn from his book of the same name, published in the UK in 2017 by Little, Brown Book Group.